Hold my lead, I've got a tail to tell

A COLLECTION OF RESCUERS STORIES OF ADOPTING A DOG

ALISON J MOORE

Alison

Preface

As you read the book, you'll notice a theme of love, patience and understanding that a rescued dog needs something special: time to develop and trust.

Many of these dogs have come from a torrid past. Immingham Dogs Home provides a lifeline for dogs in need, offering them a second chance at life. The dogs are primarily from North Lincolnshire; others were initially rescued from abroad. Some have never known what it is to be in a home environment, and others have been treated cruelly. But with the love of the rescuers, they have learnt to trust and to give and receive love and affection, even the ones that seemed to be a lost cause.

Without the tireless dedication of Kelly and Immingham Dogs Home, many of the dogs would not be here today. Kelly, in particular, loves every one of her rescues. She and her team of volunteers work exhaustingly long days to ensure the dogs are fed, exercised and loved as if they were in a home.

As for me, my partner David and I were adopted by Smudge eighteen months ago. He was, and remains a nonchalant but cocky little chap. His strange short legs on a medium-sized body give him a quirky swagger. But don't let his shortness of stature fool you. If he wants to go somewhere, he will try his damnedest to tug at the lead to get to it: I'm sure my arms are now longer than before!

Before Smudge, there was Joey, who I'll tell you about near the end of the book. He was also a rescue many years ago, and we were devastated at his loss in early 2023. Writing his story in 'Just Joey' was very cathartic, helped us move on, and made us feel good about adopting Smudge.

Following the rescuers' social media page, I read so many beautiful stories that I suggested this book idea to Kelly. I put my next project aside and began encouraging rescuers to tell their stories. We didn't know what response we would get: it could have fallen flat on its face! But slowly, we managed to coax the stories out and produce this heart-warming book.

All the stories in this book are contributions from rescuers of dogs from Immingham Dogs Home; I think we all might say that the dogs rescued us in reality!

The stories are told in the rescuers' words, conveying the warmth and love between people and their dogs.

Alycia, Ryan and Penny

After being together for seven years, we finally did it. We tied the knot, using that clichéd phrase. To stop at that would be too easy. As all newlyweds do, we embarked on a plane and spent a week on honeymoon. Two days later, we moved to an entirely new county four hours away from where we had grown up and most of my family were. We had done the significant few: marriage, a honeymoon, moving, and starting new jobs, all within two weeks of each other!

Fast-forward to our first month in our new home, and it came up again. The house was quiet. I, Ally, come from a big family. I am one of five children, with the youngest still at primary school. When Ryan was at work, there was no other sound apart from thoughts... We all know how annoying those can be! We both longed to hear the tapping of paws and the feeling of a dog's love in the house.

It was a feeling like no other. Ryan had recently lost his childhood dog, a Border Collie cross named Indi, and having had her around for most of our childhood sweetheart relationship, we knew that the first step as newlyweds was a dog.

There had been no question about rescuing. In our minds, it was the only way to get a dog. Other families we had known to rescue, and so many dogs needed a home that every dog kennel, charity or rescuing shelter our names went to.

A month passed, and still nothing. No news and no dog. We knew we wanted a 'big dog', and our dream dog would be either a German shepherd or something similar in size. A dog that could easily take up your sofa and banish you to watch telly on the floor! We kept applying, but nothing prevailed. We had the space; the surrounding area was amazing for the walks we envisaged, and we had the funds saved, ready and waiting. We didn't know it yet, but the most unique dog awaited us around the corner.

"I've done it!" Ally exclaimed.

"Done what?" Ryan questioned.

"I've applied for a dog."

"Is that because you were disappointed that Dunelm didn't have the furniture you wanted?"

"No", although sending in that application definitely restored, if not significantly multiplied, my serotonin.

Ryan was asking about the dog I had just applied for. I was sitting scrolling through social media, as everyone does as a passenger on a journey, and BBC Lincolnshire had clearly picked up on my recent searches. The article read:

'Blind Dog in race against time to find a new home'.

I saw him. He had a blue ball in his mouth, proudly showing it off like a small child proud of their new school artwork. A three-year-old German Shepherd with that traditional black and gold coat happily posing on a walk. I looked closer, and although it said blind dog, I did not think that meant he had no eyes. Two brown coloured lines sat where you would picture a dog's eyes to be. Sadly, he had lost them due to an infection. That's him, that's our dog.

Benedict was sending us a sign to come and give him the home we had prepared for him.

It couldn't have been more than an hour before my phone rang. A lady named Kelly spoke and asked about our application for Benedict. We discussed the usual T&Cs confirming details. I remember Kelly asking us when we wanted to come and see him. It was Monday, and the soonest we could get there was Friday. That was possibly the longest Monday to Friday there had ever been.

That week, we both followed the Immingham Dogs Home Facebook page and saw their post about Benedict. We were already moving our furniture around to get space for a dog's bed, deciding where a food and water bowl would go, and spending countless hours on Pets at Home and Google, researching the best toys for blind dogs.

It was Friday morning. I had just finished a night shift, running on two hours of sleep, but that would not stop us. Ryan drove, and I had a snooze in the car. I hope Benedict likes naps as much as we do, I thought as I drifted off to sleep, knowing that we would see him in just over an hour and a half.

It took us way longer than anticipated to find Immingham Dogs Home, but finally, we saw the gates. We met with Kelly and sat on the meet-and-greet sofa. Kelly had spoken to us on the phone that Monday, informing us Benedict [Benny for short] loved any toy that was a ball, so I had a tennis ball in my coat pocket and obviously some treat sticks.

We waited, hand in hand, for Benedict. The door swung open, and there he was, tail wagging, ball in mouth, bee-lining straight for us. I never really believed in love at first sight, as Ryan and I had been friends way before romance blossomed. Well, Benedict had changed that. I had never felt love like it.

We took him on a walk, and both felt very giddy. We were nervous thinking about how his blindness would affect him.

You won't believe it because a lot of believing is seeing, but Benny walked like any other dog, if not better. He navigated the world around him without a care in the world. We hope it was his way of showing he was at home.

We walked him back to Immingham and took him back to the meet-and-greet room. I remember thinking, I hope he picks us. Kelly had said Benny wasn't treat-orientated, but his nose was in my pocket as we sat. The duck treats had piqued his interest. In true Benny fashion of proving everyone wrong and defying odds, he ate three of those duck treats. It felt like he had chosen us, telling us he was ours.

Kelly packed him a hessian bag of his favourite balls and bedding that still stores his spare toys in, even now. You could see her love for him as she did it. Kelly told us that Benedict likes to have a collection of toys, all of them balls or ball-shaped, and that he will choose a new favourite each day. He would carry the 'chosen one' around until either a new ball had piqued his interest or it had gone to dog-toy ball-heaven, having to be replaced.

This amazing woman and her remarkable team had cared for Benedict, the blind German Shepherd, waiting for him to find his forever home. Kelly told us that Benedict had thought he had found his forever home but had returned because it did not work out. So we agreed that, for everyone's sake, we would wait to tell anyone about Benedict being adopted by us until a few days had passed.

Benny eagerly jumped in the back seats of our little Citroen C1. We thanked Kelly for everything, including discussing how she had people from Canada say they would come and get Benedict to give him a home! I thank Kelly every day that she thought that was too far for him to go; after all, Immingham is only a car drive away for us!

With a blind dog, we had to assess our home at Benny's level and without eyes. We rearranged our home, making sure things like the big coffee table were moved to prevent Benny from bumping into it. When we bought Benny home, we guided him around on his lead, and quickly, he knew exactly where he was. We researched the best tips and tricks to ensure each room has a different floor texture for him and that his bowls have a mat underneath to confirm where he is. Although Benny really would eat anything off wherever!

There were your typical teething problems the first few weeks as Benny got to trust and know us and vice versa. His character came out more and more. We understood that his ball is his lifeline, and he panics when he can't find it; I always think, wouldn't you if that was your comfort?

We said that dogs wouldn't be up on the sofa as we had bought a lovely new velvet sofa... that lasted for about a week before Benny fell asleep with the two of us, and he was snuggled in between.

Benny does anything for cheese, eggs, and peanut butter. He's never fussed about us eating unless we eat cheese, eggs, or peanut butter. He only ever gets dog-approved peanut butter, but if food is up for grabs, he will face you, raise his eyebrows, and give you that puppy face while drooling down your leg.

Benny has always loved balls and will always love them. We have gone through about ten already and experimented with different sizes and textures. His favourites are textured balls that are tough enough to survive the jaws of a GSD or the peanut butter-scented balls we managed to find!

Benny plays a game instead of zoomies. I won't repeat what we have called it, but it ends in off! He will hold a ball between his paws and nudge it with his nose until it pings across the floor, and then he'll chase it. He finds it by himself, too. We quickly blocked the gaps around furniture where the ball would go as if Benny were trying to find a ball; there was no stopping him from getting behind a sofa or under a table.

With rescue dogs, you have so much love to give you tend to forget that they have to adjust. It took us a good few weeks to adjust to Benny's routine. Realising what food he liked and spending money on the food he didn't [we donated it, of course!], there were a few in-house accidents, but we realised this was a poorly tummy, and probiotics sorted that out! I wouldn't say there were disasters, but the teething problems came through, and together, we listened.

We take Benny to an off-lead paddock and have found a way to play fetch with him, which he loves. We kick the ball, and the pinging sound off your foot means he can chase it and retrieve it back to you. He is honestly immensely clever.

We've bonded so much that we really feel that he is our Benedict. We talk all the time, and Benny loves Radio One. I always talk to him, and sometimes, he'll huff at me in agreement or bark to disagree. Well, it feels like he is trying to put his take on it anyway. He's not a fan of the doorbell or the ice cream van tune that comes around every Sunday.

We've taught Benny to drop, and sometimes other dogs on walks spook him a bit, so we're getting better at being calm with them day by day. Benny's made doggie friends in the neighbourhood, and everyone recognises him. He attracts everyone, and everyone wants to say hi and understand him more and more.

Benny has been our saviour, and it's true that dogs truly are our best friends. We cherish him more and more. We don't know what life is like without him now.

We also keep in touch with the family that fostered Benny before we adopted him, and thank them so much for looking after him until we found him!

Immingham gave us the missing piece to our family, and we can't thank them enough for all the work and dedication they show. Without them, we wouldn't have met Benedict, the love of our life.

Georgina, Rick and Gusti

Picture this: Nine-year-old me walking home from school and being greeted by the wagging smile of a doggos tail. My nanna passed her to me after we had sadly lost her. Suzie was a twelve-year-old fox terrier cross. She was my shadow and my first best friend, even with the budding weight issue caused by treats!

My favourite part of any day was seeing that fuzz ball waddling through to greet me, building memories and forming who I am today. She taught me responsibility, loyalty and how to express love and compassion without words.

Some people say they are just dogs. I disagree; they are staples of who you become.

Fast-forward to being a responsible adult with a mortgage, three cats, a small human, and a job, which means my husband and I are ships that pass in the night. Adding to the madness of the home is a fantastic idea. Who wouldn't want their child to share that same joy I had as a child? I guess the inner child inside also missed that wagging tail greeting you each day.

After talking with a friend at work, the idea was planted that maybe it was time to look for a furry walking partner, and at this point, it was just an idea. However, after receiving a few tags on Facebook for some likely candidates, my newsfeed soon had a mind of its own. Before I knew it, pups were popping up everywhere. But there was no rush, and we needed to be sure that we welcomed the right doggo into our life and onto our sofa.

Then imagine Him. Those brown eyes that show you into his soul and the thought of that wagging tail! [Although lacking some length]. He was perfect! The photo was nothing spectacular. A brown dog in a field [questionably the size of a miniature Shetland Pony], but something about this creature made me know he needed to come home and share the love of this family. I started picturing how he would fit into our lives, how he would fit on our sofa! But I knew for sure he would quite easily fit by my side.

So, I sent in an enquiry, questioning what he would be like with the cats and what they would think of him. And would you believe it? He loves cats, and I had the honour of meeting him.

That was it, I saw him, my beautiful Gusti goo. I couldn't leave him; he looked so big yet so small and fragile as soon as he looked at you with those big, brown, heart-melting eyes. Before I knew it, he was snug and safe in the back of the car.

When I met Gusti, I was told a little of his story. They believed him to be some sort of gun dog; he was around eighteen months to two years old. He had been found by the side of the road in Romania. He had come over to the UK recently and had only just arrived at Immingham just before I had.

On the drive home, I had a moment of panic. I questioned all my life choices as the K9 equivalent of a donkey drooled down my arm. What was I doing? What would my husband Rick say when he was presented with our housemate that I was just 'going to meet'?

When we got home, he was nervous and reserved, which I fully expected; he spent a good couple of hours exploring cautiously. I'd made him a bed under the stairs so he had a safe hiding space until he felt comfortable. That didn't take him too long; by the time I'd picked my daughter up from school, he wanted to play with his new toys.

Although it was only small glimpses, we were quickly seeing his personality. A goofy boy who wanted to play. I noticed he wouldn't leave me far; he was always by my side. He was my shadow!

Up until this point, my husband had still not met Gusti; he had received a video with a message demanding he bring some meat home with him to welcome the new addition. That night, I put my daughter to bed and sat on the sofa with my new buddy at my feet, watching TV and relishing how well this had worked out, how I couldn't have come home with a more perfect dog if I'd designed him myself.

The growling started when the front door opened, and his posture changed... It had never crossed my mind that meeting a man would be an issue. Gusti instantly went into protective mode. In hindsight, I think it was a rooky mistake on my behalf; he'd not met my husband, and then this man just appeared in our house late at night.

After an awkward hour or two of trying to convince Gusti that Rick wouldn't hurt us, steal the TV, or eat all the dog biscuits, we put Gusti to bed, not really knowing what to expect. But after a little cry, he settled and was an angel!

The next morning, I was greeted by the waggiest bum I had ever seen! It took us a little while for Gusti to feel comfortable with men, mops, bottles or loud noises, but fast forward to now, and he has the waggiest tale for everyone who we welcome in [even if he does the biggest bark to notify someone is at the door]. I can only imagine the life he had before his life with us, but it's irrelevant now because, in our house, he is the king!

In the following days, I was contacted by the fantastic lady, Stella, who had rescued him in Romania. She told me his story, how her husband had found him so scared and starving by the side of the road that he seemed as though he'd never seen love. The photos of him when he was first rescued broke my heart.

I will be forever grateful for all the amazing work Stella did with him, just so we had the opportunity to have this gentle-natured, beautiful-souled, goofy boy a place in our home. A year and a half later, I'm still as obsessed with him as I was at the start. That floppy-eared, cuddle monkey can do no wrong. He is living his best life when he's in a blanket, looking like ET!

We have had some challenges thrown our way that I honestly don't think I could have overcome without the help of my hairy companion. Gusti's confidence has grown insanely. Everyone who meets him can't help but fall a little bit in love with him. He still thinks the cats will protect him from the postie. This huge, adorable bundle of love and fun couldn't have found us at a better time. He has become everyone's support when they need a moment or a well-timed wake-yourself trump to cheer them up.

I find it fascinating that a creature so far removed from humans can be understanding, empathetic and compassionate in a way most people are unable to comprehend.

Around a year ago, I was diagnosed with a brain tumour. Gusti has seen it all and stayed by my side throughout. For every breakdown, he's laid on the kitchen floor and laid with me, his nose on my cheek. Every day spent napping and resting, he was there with cuddles and a look of pure love. He even stayed with me through my first seizure, refusing to leave until I got up.

This incredible fluff ball will probably never understand the full impact he has on my life. The bond I share with Gusti is something I didn't expect when I was just looking for a walking buddy, a playmate for my daughter and a heart for our home. I'm not sure when it happened, but we became a unit; we all understand each other's needs.

Gusti and my husband have an amazing bond. It took a lot of work and patience for Rick, but it was like one day, something clicked, and these two old souls found comfort in each other's company. Gusti seemed to feel settled and safe.

As I sit and think of how the Gusti chapter of our lives came to be, there is a part of me that believes some things are just meant to be. For us, it was that this sofa-hogging, cover-stealing pooch belonged with us.

Disclaimer: My husband will now question that I favour the dog more than him. I would very much like to point out that I would never say this out loud!

Rachael, Paul, Alyssa, Tristan and Frankie

My daughter Alyssa has always loved animals.

Alyssa has an autistic condition, which means she has a different understanding of how to socialise with people. She is friendly and polite but does not crave human interaction to the level of the majority of society.

Alyssa, like her brother Tristan, grew up with animals from birth. As she got older, we lost our first dog and went on to have two Romanian rescues before Immingham Dogs Home was established. Alyssa gets upset when we lose any of her pets but takes pleasure in the fact that she believes they are all playing together in heaven.

I noticed a post on Facebook and messaged Kelly at the rescue. I explained everything about Alyssa and how she would like to volunteer. Alyssa was fourteen at the time. That very same day, she went to the rescue and walked her first rescue dogs.

The dogs make Alyssa feel happy, and she loves taking care of them. Alyssa loves dogs and would have as many as she could, but I say three large dogs are enough. She loves going to the dog shelter and actually gets really happy when they get a home.

Over the next few years, we raised money by doing sponsored car washes, completing a 5k assault course, and volunteering on behalf of Immingham Dogs Home at a pet store to raise awareness of the shelter. We were also interviewed by Look North about our volunteering at the shelter. Alyssa has also taken the photos of the dogs for the Immingham Dogs Home calendar.

Over the years, the whole family have been weekly volunteers. We have even had a few sleep overs and taken some of the dogs out on daytrips.

We have walked many dogs but have never adopted another, as we have a dominant resident dog who isn't very accepting of new dogs. Late one night, Kelly posted about the need for an emergency foster home for Frankie, who had been returned that day through no fault of his own, and he was really struggling. Frankie is a living Scooby Doo and submissive.

Frankie had always been a family favourite. He was suffering an injury and needed somewhere to settle and rest. We immediately contacted Kelly, and she asked if we were sure, considering Shula, our dominant dog. We said we would make it work, and with the help of a spare crate from Kelly, we brought Frankie home.

Frankie is a gentle giant. Shula accepted that he wasn't a threat, and Amber, our other dog, accepted him straight away. He has got a strange obsession with wet towels! He loves to whip them off his humans and roll around on them. When he's finished, he just tosses them to one side!

Amber is a collie cross, and we got her as a playmate for Shula before Immingham Dogs Home was established. She is the eldest of the pack and has lived with us since she was two and is seven years old.

Shula is a Labrador cross and is the most traumatised but the dominant dog. She arrived with us at seven months from Romania and had spent her whole life being chased and attacked by angry villagers. Only her mum and one pup other than her survived. She lived with our resident dog, Molly, who was thirteen, but sadly, we lost her only four months after getting Shula, hence the arrival of Amber. Shula is five now and has struggled with new people and other dogs since growing up through COVID.

We also have a stray cat called Sneezy. When we found him around nine years ago, he was on death's door; he's still going well since we got him and nursed him back to health.

Frankie went from coming to us for emergency foster care to now being in his permanent home.

Polly, Trish and Tia

On 16th August 2023, Tia came for a sleepover...and never returned; this is Tia's story.

Sadly, our mum passed away in September 2022, and we felt lost and needed to find a purpose again. We are twin sisters. In April 2023, we saw an advert on social media for volunteer dog walkers for Immingham Dogs Home. We both love dogs and have been dog owners previously, so we rang to volunteer.

We weren't looking for a dog. We just loved walking the dogs and spending time with them. We even took some of them for days out to the beach and had some for sleepovers.

We first saw Tia in the playroom when we were taking some of the other dogs for their walks. She came over to see us, had a little fuss, and then ate her treat outside.

The second meeting was when she won Best Rescue at the Immingham Dog Show.

We were due to go on holiday in August 2023 and asked Kelly if we could take a couple of the dogs out again for the day when we got back. Kelly suggested Tia, who was nine years old and hadn't been out before. She explained to us that Tia was from Romania, and when she came to the Home, her teeth were terrible, and she was suffering. She was taken to the vet to have some of her teeth removed, and she became a different girl.

Our understanding of Tia's circumstances was that she was a street dog who had been picked up to be used as bait for dog fighting before she was saved.

Throughout the holiday, we both could not stop thinking about this nine-year-old girl looking for her forever home. As soon as we returned, we messaged Kelly to see if we could take her to the beach.

On 14th August, we took her to the beach, and she was amazing. We both warmed to her instantly, even though it cost me [Polly] a new phone. She ran towards the sea, decided she didn't like it and ran out. In the furore, my phone dropped out of my pocket and fell into the sea!

After we took her back, all we could think about was her and that this girl needed a home, so we contacted Kelly again and asked if we could take Tia for a sleepover.

We both live in flats on the same site, so we took her to both, and she settled in both immediately. Kelly told us that she was an 'anything goes girl' and was really easy-going, and she showed us this.

We took her out to the park, and we could see she loved spending time with us. We all stayed in one flat that night to be with her. She got straight on the bed and fell fast asleep as if she was home already. We asked Kelly if she could stay with us for a few more nights, and Kelly suggested fostering her. We jumped at the chance as we had both already considered adopting her.

We did find it challenging to find something she liked to eat; she turned her nose up at most food, and we mean turned her nose up! She would look at the food, then turn her head away and stick her nose in the air as if to say, 'I'm not eating that'. We eventually learnt that Tia would eat if we hand-fed her, and still, to this day, we are hand-feeding her. She likes to get on the sofa in a comfy position, and then we are allowed to feed her. This may be that people used to hand feed her when she was on the streets, or she is just a bit of a diva and has us both wrapped around her little paw. She never says no to her favourite doggy treats, though, piggies in blankets.

On 1st September 2023, we officially adopted Tia, and this was when Tia got her **two** forever homes and her two Mummies: Mummy P and Mummy T. It was almost overnight that her personality and character really started to come out.

She started walking quicker, and her head began to rise. It didn't take long to see her perform zoomies, either.

Tia settled in really quickly when moving from one flat to another, and Kelly did say this about her. Well, this means she has four sofas to choose from, which is a bonus for her as she is a sofa girlie.

After the first two weeks, we had to return to work, so we bought pet cameras for each flat to monitor her. She barked when we left our flats, which worried us in case she couldn't settle without us there. We persevered, and this only happened for a couple of weeks, and then she soon got used to the routine.

We have found that Tia can act like a stroppy teenager [for those of you who can remember Kevin and Perry, then picture that]. If we try to take her outside for her last wee-wee before bedtime, she will have a strop and throw herself around; we must admit it is quite funny to watch.

Tia has Jack Russell in her, which explains her stubbornness. If she doesn't want to do anything, she sticks her paws into the ground, her nose up in the air, and looks away from you.

Tia seems to think that paths are hers and that no other dogs are allowed on them while she is walking. She barks at most dogs. We did enrol her in dog training, but she still does it. We are still working on this.

Tia loves to play on the grass. She can stand up one minute and then flop herself over the next so she can have a good belly rub. She does look like a drama queen when she does this, though. We have found that Tia does not entertain toys. She likes to play with dog puzzles, but only because they have treats in them.

In the beginning, we registered her at the vet, and the vet estimated her age as 4 to 6 years old. Kelly had always said her passport says nine years old, but she thought more five to six years so she was spot on. He also said she did not look like a rescue as she was well looked after and her teeth were good; this was a big credit to Immingham Dog Home.

When she went back to the vet for a booster some months later, the vet put the needle in, and she ran off around the room with the needle still in her. She never barked or snapped, though, and eventually let the vet take it out.

Tia is not a fan of the bath. It becomes a two-woman job. We have to put her harness on as she does a runner around the flat to try and hide. Once she has been washed, she loves the towel drying and will happily sit in her dressing gown.

Everyone who meets Tia falls in love with her. She is really good around humans and loves to be fussed over. She loves her grandad [our dad]; when he walks with us, she constantly nudges his hand to stroke her.

We have been lucky with Tia, as she settled in straight away and hasn't caused us any issues. She is perfect, and the best thing we have ever done was adopt her. When she looks at us with her beautiful eyes, she just melts us. We rescued her, but really, she rescued us.

David, Alison & Smudge

We had recently lost our wonderful dog, Joey. He was an amazing nineteen-year-old and had been my companion for nine years after his previous owner had died: he had been my saviour. When I met David, he fell in love with him too. Joey loved having a man around the house and followed David everywhere, much to my chagrin!

Our life felt empty when we lost Joey, although he was only a small, reasonably quiet dog who you didn't realise was there a lot of the time. We left his beds in place in the lounge and the bedroom and daily mourned his passing. The house was too quiet without a dog to love and be loved by. Even though we were heartbroken, we knew Joey would be happy for us to give a home to a rescue dog, so we began looking.

We scoured so many rehoming sites that dogs were becoming a blur. Young ones, old ones, breeding bitches that had been rescued from horrid circumstances, and ones that needed rescuing from other countries. There were so many choices that it was overwhelming, and I certainly felt the pressure of making the right choice for the dog we would have.

We both liked the look of a pair of rescued breeding cocker spaniel bitches, so with trepidation, David booked a visit to see them. They were lovely girls. Very friendly and loving. It was so sad that neither of them reacted to their names or knew what to do with the myriad of toys scattered around for them. They would wander in and out, wagging their tails and coming to us for a fuss. Unfortunately, they had no toilet training and were peeing on the lounge floor of the house at the rescue centre.

As we left the rescue centre to decide, my heart broke. I cried all the way home. I was still raw from the loss of Joey and wasn't ready yet to take on another dog, let alone two. With a heavy heart, I silenced all the rescue centres on Facebook for thirty days and tried to forget about another dog until I felt I was grieving less from losing Joey. All I wanted was my boy back.

After thirty days, the rescue centres started popping up again on my feed. I was definitely feeling better; my broken heart was slowly mending. I looked back for the cocker bitches, but they had gone. I smiled and hoped they had gone to a good home with someone who could give them the time they needed.

Meanwhile, David sat in one room on his computer, and I in another. Both of us searched through many, many dogs. Then I said to David I was going to send him a link. I pinged it across to him, and when he opened it, he exclaimed, "I've just been looking at him."

I entered David's office, and we both sat there looking at this quirky black bundle of floof with the shortest legs we had ever seen. Think of a border collie crossed with a corgi and you have Smudge! His photos showed him with other dogs and on the beach having fun. There was also one photo of him up on his hind legs. He was so cute. "Do you think he could be the one?"

We called Kelly, filled out all the necessary paperwork, and waited. Meanwhile, we were both scouring the Facebook page for more pictures of him! We still looked at other dogs, but none looked more suitable than Smudge.

Kelly contacted us very quickly and arranged a meet-and-greet. At this time, we also had a long chat with Tia, who had fostered him. She gave us a great insight into his foibles and personality.

When meet-and-greet day arrived, two very nervous adults drove over to meet Smudge. As we pulled into the rescue, David said, "Look, there he is," and pointed to where he was, up on the windowsill of Kelly's conservatory, barking his head off! I felt sick. I hoped I wasn't going to bail out this time.

Kelly popped his harness on and brought him out to meet us. He certainly was a little weirdo! His body was large on his little legs, and he had so much fur that he looked fat! I bent down to say hello and soon realised he wasn't fat at all; it was all floof. We went into the garden, and Kelly let him off his lead.

We had come prepared with treats in our pockets, and once we had ok'd it with Kelly, I offered him a treat. Treat taken; he assumed we were ok and rolled onto his back for a belly rub. Once he had enough of that, he got up, wandered around the garden, and completely ignored us.

David asked me what I thought. "I love him," I said. "We can give him a good home." Meanwhile, Smudge came back for more treats and belly rubs.

Our only problem was that we had two weeks of holidays booked, and we asked if Kelly was happy to hold on to him for us till then. None of us wanted to drag him from one stable environment into another home, a motorhome and different locations within days of having him.

So, we said goodbye for now and headed home. Looking forward to having Smudge at home with us did both of us a power of good: it was like planning for a new baby!

The next day, we were off to the pet store for a crate, as Smudge likes his own space. Of course, a crate turned into treats and a couple of toys to make him feel he was home. We moved Joey's bed into my office. As it was a big cushion type, Smudge could use that one, too, if he wanted to. He wouldn't be restricted as to where he could go. Then we made up Smudge's crate where the cushion had been and plonked the orange octopus toy on his bed. Now we waited.

This space, from saying yes to actually getting Smudge, was therapeutic. It gave me time to balance things out in my head with the transition from Joey to Smudge being in the home. Smudge was so different from Joey, and that was a good thing.

When we returned from our holiday, we were eager to collect Smudge. We had told everyone we had met up with about him. In my head, I often talked to Joey about him, too, especially when I was on my own. It reassured me that we were doing the right thing.

The following day, we were off. The doggy seatbelt was clipped into the back, and a blanket was put on the seats. It only then occurred to me that Smudge might not be able to jump into the car with his little legs! Ah, well, we could sort that out when the time came.

We arrived at Immingham Dogs Home, and once more, there was Smudge, barking at the conservatory window: not a boy to be ignored this one. We were all excited, I think!

Smudge came out with his natural bossy character, and once David took his lead, he decided to chase the black cat! David was caught unaware and almost pulled off his feet! Smudge saw it all as a game.

We opened the car door, and we needn't have worried. Smudge leapt straight in and sat there doing a happy pant. Clipped in, we said goodbye to Kelly and headed for home. Smudge happily sat in the back seat, watching the world go by.

Kelly had warned us that he was an eager beaver to leave the car. Thank heavens for the seat belt! He really couldn't wait! It was then that I realised how strong he is. It was a battle of wills to hold onto his harness, clip on his lead, and unclip his seat belt!

We let him off in the garden, and he had a good sniff around before marking his territory. Opening the house door, he soon came in to explore. He seemed very confident. We gave him a treat. He sniffed at his crate, went in, and lay down. We sat down with a cup of tea and just looked. You never know what to expect, but going straight to sleep in a new crate and bed, wasn't it!

His first walk around the block was telling. Smudge on a lead was a nightmare! At the end of the first week, my wrists and arms were killing me. I was being pulled all over the place. Where Smudge wanted to go, he went. If he didn't go, he sat or lay down on the spot and refused to budge.

We left Smudge downstairs in his crate with the door open the first night. Previous dogs had slept in the bedroom, so this was a strange feeling for us. Good as gold, he stayed downstairs all night. When we woke up, I called his name. It took only a few seconds before we heard his claws on the floor downstairs, pattering towards the staircase. A very noisy thunder of paws came upstairs, and, in the half-light, this big black buffoon jumped onto our bed!

He was so pleased with himself that his crazy tail was wagging into a blur.

We soon realised that Smudge is a very vocal dog. He barks, and then he will bark some more. He still has a verbal battle with the neighbour's dogs, but at least they aren't trying to rip the fence down in between the gardens any more [well, not too often]. It's just like having a frank exchange of words between them.

We found that Smudge wouldn't jump up on the furniture unless encouraged to do so [or when we were out sometimes]. Someone had trained him really well in the house: he was a darling. But boy, when he did come up onto the sofa, he would sit as close as he could. He does love his cuddles. So much so that he has now perfected the 'half-pike twist'. If I sit in the chair, he will jump front paws onto my chest and twist his bum in mid-air to land himself in my lap. He is such a funny boy.

It was a few months before we heard him growl when he was sitting by David in the motorhome. We both stopped chatting and wondered why he was growling. But he was talking! The talking became a regular thing and has become more frequent, especially when he knows it's food time. He likes to play with his toys just before and is keen for us to be a part of that. He also began to look at us in the eye rather than looking down. Then he would smile, showing his lovely white teeth. If dogs did toothpaste adverts, he would be the perfect star.

We took delivery of a new motorhome, which had been planned before Smudge came along. It had a large, side-opening door and a flyscreen that you could draw across. As we had gotten to know Smudge a lot better, we figured he would happily sit inside behind the flyscreen. How wrong could we be? We drew the flyscreen across, and Smudge just pushed at the bottom and went outside! We hadn't tested his recall, which we knew was dubious, but I called his name, and he came straight back in as good as gold. One disaster of a lost dog averted. A board now runs across the gap to stop this from happening again!

* * *

We have had Smudge for over twelve months now, and he has continued to become more settled. His barking at everything that moves is much less as he grows more confident in his surroundings, and he loves being let off on the beach at Cleethorpes.

The first time we let him off, we were scared stiff he would do a runner. [Joey would have bolted!] But he was good as gold and enjoyed sniffing around and chatting to other dogs. A lady with a Border Collie and a ball came from further up the beach. She threw the ball, and off went Smudge after it! How embarrassing. But she said it was fine, and the two dogs played happily for half an hour as we watched. It was lovely to see him so happy, as he doesn't bother with balls at home.

Smudge is now settled into the family. He sleeps wherever he wants, often coming up to bed with us and, after a fuss, going back onto the floor to prop his head up the bed and go to sleep. He tends to move around the room at night and rarely sleeps on his bed, preferring the floor. Occasionally, he will go downstairs to sleep or have a drink and then return. There are times when I go to bed before David. Smudge waits until I give the command to jump on the bed, then snuggles immediately on David's side. He won't engage with you at all at this point. I'm sure he thinks that if he ignores you, you won't think he is there! Dogs are weird.

He is less wary of strangers and unknown dogs now, too. In fact, he can be an embarrassment on campsites as he pulls towards people sitting outside and won't budge until he has had a fuss. Although his loud bark can make some people fearful of him, I don't see that as a bad thing. He is incredibly protective of us, the home, and the motorhome.

He even enjoys going to see Jess at the groomers! Now that all his dew claws are well clipped, he actually enjoys the experience-especially the bath and being blow-dried! Our rufty-tufty fellow loves a bit of pampering.

I'm sure Joey would be happy that we took the plunge and gave Smudge a new home.

Jason & Faye

Faye was rehomed from Amicii at Immingham in 2020. She was a nervous, gentle soul that had been waiting for a home for some time.

After a very difficult life in Romania, she was scared of everything. After losing our beloved Scamp, we had space in our lives and our homes, and we welcomed Faye with open hearts. Over the short time she had with us, her confidence grew, as did her voice.

She would let us know very loudly if she was unhappy or wanted treats!

Suddenly, in early 2021, we lost Faye after a very short illness. We were absolutely heartbroken. The year we had with her was too short but so sweet. As sad as we still feel some years later, she brought joy to our hearts, watching her confidence and happiness slowly grow as she accepted us into her life.

Liz and Xavi

If I remember correctly, our first thought when we saw a picture of Xavi was that it must be a photo of him when they first rescued him. He was very matted and sad-looking. It said he had been reserved, but I could not stop thinking about him.

We were still going through our checks and had our interview booked, but then my friend [who has rescued two from Immingham] contacted me to say he was back up and needed a forever home.

I called and was told this was correct, and I asked if we could come to meet him. We travelled as an excited family to Immingham, and we all fell in love. He was very needy and liked females over males.

The first few nights were interesting. I don't think he had ever slept in his own bed. He wanted to be close to me. I must have put him back in his bed about twenty times; It made me feel like a new mum again.

I left him for a few hours the first time to see how he would behave. When I returned home, he had eaten most of my blinds and was very distressed.

I contacted the lady in Spain who had taken him off the streets. She informed me he had lived with an elderly lady that had died in the house. He had been locked in with two other large dogs, which they think had attacked him [he has half an ear missing]. He managed to escape and then spent some time on the streets of Alicante.

He now spends some days with my mum when I am at work. They both potter about the garden and have afternoon naps together. We are now up to about four hours, with him being okay to leave. He is the most wonderful, loving dog and now enjoys spending time with my husband and son. But he still prefers me, which I love. Sometimes, the universe lines you up for a reason, and our reason is Xavi.

Jane, Nicholas, Ruby and Oscar [Lewis]

Sadly, our family were victims of a fatal dog-on-dog attack where we lost our beloved pet, Ruby. Ruby was my son's emotional support animal, and while walking her one evening, a loose, large dog appeared out of nowhere from an open gateway and took Ruby's life. We were devastated to lose her in such an unexpected and cruel way.

My son was utterly devastated. He has a rare autoimmune condition and has had to overcome some truly shattering symptoms. He developed special educational needs after his illness [PANS, Paediatric Acute-Onset Neuropsychiatric Syndrome].

Ruby was his best friend. She slept in his bed and sat at his desk in his room. They rarely left each other's side. Ruby's death plunged Nicholas into depression. He could no longer attend his education setting and was angry and lost.

Oscar came into our lives not to replace Ruby because no dog could ever do that, but we still had such love to give. We feel like Ruby brought Oscar into our lives and that we could give a rescue dog a second chance at being loved. Ruby was taken too soon, and Oscar had years to give. Our paths crossed, and we agreed to give Oscar as much love as we still had left after losing Ruby.

Oscar [previously named Lewis] was petrified of everything. He was very anxious about men, but he seemed to trust Nicholas, my son, really quickly. Oscar snuggled up to Nicholas on the way home, and he allowed Nicholas into his personal space.

It hasn't been easy, but as each week passes, Oscar has settled some more. His unique, quirky ways make us laugh, but he's revealed that our bond has strengthened by being shown patience, respect, and space. We still have work to do, but he no longer barks at the light switch being flicked in the next room.

Nicholas loves to take him to a local secure dog park, and our other dog has taught him to play. It's lovely to see the two dogs interacting and initiating play. They both read each other's body language really well.

We still miss Ruby immensely, but Oscar has helped us on our grieving journey. He's helping us as much as we're helping him. Nicholas is slowly progressing with his studies and participating in new hobbies. Oscar has been as much our saviour as we are his.

Jo, Dave, Luke & Rosie

Dave and I had always wanted a dog throughout our married life, and our son Luke always wanted one, too. We had not got one before because we were both out at work and school every day. Then, our circumstances changed, and I began to work from home. We wanted Luke to have the experience of having a dog, as Dave and I had fond memories and funny stories of family dogs as we grew up. Matt, my white Labrador, and Dave's Trixie, who was black and tan. Luke had grown up with the two rescue dogs of his grandparents: Bruce and [another] Trixie.

We knew we wanted to adopt a rescue dog and started looking at online sites. We found a 'Kevin' and a 'Laddie' and then came across Noah's Ark and rescue dogs from Romania. There were photos of puppies that had been rescued with their mum, the puppies were Bonnie, Jasmine and Rosie. It happened very quickly, as we completed the application at the beginning of the week and spoke to Vanda at Noah's Ark. Luke was to have responsibility for this new addition to our family, so he prepared the video of our house and garden for the checking process, and Vanda was impressed that he had done such a good thorough job. We made a list of what this puppy would need. We were told that the puppies were at Immingham Dogs Home, which was very close to where we lived, and that we could go and meet Kelly and the puppies on the Friday. We were all so excited.

Luke and I were keen on the blond puppy Bonnie, and Dave secretly liked the black and tan of Jasmine and Rosie because they reminded him of his dog Trixie. The puppies were five and a half months old, so they were not small. Kelly informed me that one of the puppies had been brought back after being adopted for a short while. I informed Kelly that no matter what, the puppy we adopted would not return to the kennels.

All the puppies came for a fuss. Bonnie and Jasmine were very energetic and bouncy, and they clambered all over Luke. They then went off to play. Rosie was a bit smaller and stayed with me and then with Dave longer. I said they were all gorgeous and wanted them all. Kelly said, 'I think you have been chosen', nodding at Rosie, and Dave agreed. Luke and I agreed. We were going to adopt Rosie because she had adopted us. Kelly asked if we were going to take her home that evening. We didn't have a thing ready, so we agreed to collect Rosie early the next morning because Kelly was supporting her daughter, who was doing a skydive to raise funds for the Immingham Dogs Home.

That evening, we went to the pet store, and Dave laughed as the first items Luke and I put in the basket were a toy burger, a toy elephant with crinkly ears, and two toy doughnuts: priorities! We soon filled the basket with bowls, a collar and lead, shampoo, and food. Dave picked a big crate, which I said was going to be too big, but it isn't because Rosie now fills it when she is laid down!

On the morning, we collected Rosie, we were all very excited and a bit apprehensive that she was going to be able to settle with us. We knew it was going to take time for Rosie to feel at home and relax. Rosie was petrified and shaking when we put her in the back seat of the car. Luke sat with her, talked to her reassuringly, and gave her a cuddle. Rosie did not like the car at all and would not go near it or in it for weeks afterwards. Luckily, we were not far from home. When we got there, we played with her in the garden and fed her by hand using her name. We kept her name because this name means a lot to us: our Nannie's middle name was Rose, and it was October, which was near to Nannie's birthday and the anniversary of her passing.

Rosie was interested in her toys and liked sniffing and exploring the garden. She lay out on the floor a lot and was introduced to her crate, which she eventually went in and laid down. Rosie liked going for walks and was great on the lead as the kennels had taken the puppies out on walks. In the first couple of weeks, we were out for a walk in the village and crossed the road as a man was walking towards us with an adult dog that we thought was a rottweiler. On introduction, the man, Kevin, who was a volunteer dog walker for the kennels, shouted over, 'Is that Rosie?' We said that we had just adopted her, and he told us that he used to walk Rosie regularly and that the adult dog he was walking was Rosie's mum. Mum and Rosie met, and Mum sniffed and checked Rosie all over. It was a lovely moment, and we took photographs of Rosie at six months old with her mum.

We discovered that Rosie was a very clean girl and only had a couple of accidents in the house until she knew which door led outside. Rosie demonstrated lots of funny and strange sleeping positions, which we learned is typical of a Rommie. We particularly liked the 'one leg and paw in the air' sleeping position or laid out with only her back legs in the dog basket. She liked her toys, particularly a toy carrot and fell in love with Gran and Grandad, who always had treats.

Rosie enjoyed walks and the good life, sleeping on the sofa, particularly upside down. She liked her space and quickly loved her crate, which was her safe space where no one bothered her. She liked pinching socks and barking at the next-door's chickens. Rosie is intelligent and knows her own mind. We took her to puppy classes with a local dog trainer, and she learnt how to walk to heel and socialise with other young dogs and how to do tricks. Dave practised her training with her every day: sit/wait/turn/touch.

Luke taught her to give paws and jump on and jump off, and I went to a training class to teach Rosie to recall on a long line. One week, Rosie achieved 'Puppy of the Week' and got a star for her progress. We were very proud. However, because she is a clever girl, she quickly learnt how to open doors and the baby gate; we had to keep her safe. She knew which parts of the mechanism to chew on the baby gate, and eventually, it didn't work properly. She chewed her toys, and their ears, arms, legs, or tails disappeared. She dug a hole in the garden; it looked like she was trying to make a well. She helped with gardening by taking the picked weeds out of the bucket and throwing them back around the garden!

From puppy to teenager, Rosie was a challenge. She became very lively from 8 pm every evening, and she liked to zoom around the living room for a couple of hours. She liked to scratch the living room carpet [and still does]. We took her for lengthy walks daily, but they did not seem to reduce her energy level. She was a bit of a bully, too. We went to an experienced dog trainer who completed some training sessions with Rosie. His conclusion was that 'Rosie is a difficult dog' because she is intelligent, knows her own mind, and is defiant, not always wanting to please her owner! We love Rosie. However, we did not like some of her behaviours, and no matter what we did to try and understand and resolve, her behaviours would continue, or new ones would appear.

Well, the time passed, and we celebrated Rosie's 1st, 2nd and 3rd birthdays. She had some more training, and we all persevered as a pack, trying to understand, learn and get along. It took a long time and period of adjustment for us all, and Rosie became calmer. We've had lots of fun times with Rosie: she laid down in the arena when we entered her for her first fun dog show. She now lays on the sofa or at my feet while I work. She loves going out in the car and can't wait to jump in. She plays with her toys rather than destroying them, and she has her favourite ones. We've had fun times at the beach as she loves to run into the sea and then run back and jump at you, so you get wet too! We have met up with the owner of Rosie's sibling Jasmine, who is now Lola, and we meet up regularly for long walks with Rosie and Lola to compare notes, stories, and advice on bringing up and looking after these crazy girls!

These days, we laugh more at Rosie's behaviours than we get frustrated. We've all been on a journey, which hasn't always been easy, but we are proud that we kept our promise to Kelly that Rosie would never go back to the kennels because she's our girl, and we love her so much.

Pat, Steve, Billybobs & Olly [Bear]

All our 50 years plus of married life, we have had rescue dogs. We have had different breeds, shapes, and sizes, and all have been a joy to have and brought so much joy, love and happiness to our lives.

After losing our last dog and the heartbreak it brings, we decided a few years ago to go a while without one. We fulfilled our retirement dream and decided to live a little time abroad, so we moved to Turkey for a while. We had decided we were not going to have any more four-legged friends so we could explore and see the country.

However, we had only been there a few days, and Elli, as we called her, decided we were her new friends. We were followed by Pup, who we rescued as he needed a vet and then had to be kept inside to avoid infection.

Inevitably, he became our second Turkish dog. About three years later, Floss arrived at the end of the street, virtually unconscious and dehydrated. We took her in, too. And then there were three.

We returned to England after eight years away, and of

course, Elli, Pup and Floss came back with us. Sadly, since then, we have lost Elli and Pup and have only Floss. Floss is such a beautiful, placid, friendly dog, but she did not settle too well as an only dog. She has always had a friend living with her. We were so upset at the loss of our lovely girl and boy but couldn't see Floss depressed as a lone dog. After a lot of soul-searching and weighing up all the pros and cons, we started looking for a friend for Floss.

We were both looking online for a friend and the practicalities of what sort of rescue would be best. I finally came upon the Immingham Dogs Home [which we didn't even know existed until then]. After contacting them, we were soon on our way to find a friend for Floss.

With Floss in the car, we made our way to Immingham. Unfortunately, on this occasion, none were suitable for one reason or another. We were so disappointed, as was Kelly, and then she asked us if we would consider an older dog than we had been looking at. Of course, we said yes, which is when we met Bobby.

He was such a friendly, happy boy, and he and Floss immediately hit it off. We had found a friend for Floss, after all. Bobby is a very happy and 'smiley' Springer Spaniel who is adorable and full of life and fun. He was the opposite of Floss, who, coming up twelve, was slowing down but still had her moments.

Within hours of their meeting, it was as if they had known each other all their lives. Kelly had said she thought Bobby was around nine years old. He settled well in the car and was happy to explore the back garden as soon as we got home.

We had been home for about ten minutes, just got a coffee in our hands and splash! Bobby had found the small pond at the bottom of the garden. We had never really known how deep it was, but the previous house owner told us it was about a foot deep. Bobby couldn't manage to get out on his own, so Steve had to give him a helping hand. Although the pond was very small, it was actually about three feet deep! We decided it would be easier to fill it in rather than find a way to keep Bobby out, so it quickly became a rockery.

Bobby, now called Billybobs, settled in so fast and so well, and we couldn't believe the bond between him and Floss. His papers came through, and we found he was actually eleven years old, but it didn't matter. He was still our boy and Flossie's forever friend.

We had a couple of short-stay holidays booked, so I rang the people and asked if we could increase the number of dogs to two for our stay. There was no problem there, so off we went to a cottage in Levisham, near the Hole of Horcum in Yorkshire.

We all enjoyed the walks and the countryside and even took the dogs on a train to Pickering. This was a big adventure for them, especially Billybobs, who sat on my knee watching all the scenery through the train window.

We spent a whole day walking in the Hole of Horcum. While resting with a drink and bite to eat, I accidentally let go of Billybobs lead, and he bolted and found the stream over the ridge where we were sitting.

Splash!

He was off like a shot, and Steve had to jump in after him to grab his lead. Billybobs love of water had got the better of him, and he was loving it. I was calling him but couldn't hear him or Steve. After what seemed an age, a very wet Billybobs came over the ridge and behind him, my dripping wet hubby! I didn't know whether to laugh or cry. If we had lost him, we would have been devastated.

Fortunately, Steve caught up with him as his lead had caught on a rock, which stopped him from going further. Knowing how quickly a situation can change, we vowed to keep a tight hold on him in future. Due to his love of water, we decided to buy him a paddling pool on our return home, and he loved being in that!

Our next short break took us to a cottage near Filey; of course, Billybobs loved the sea. We couldn't keep him out, so we had no choice but to go in with him on his extending lead. Paddling up to our knees in seawater was worth it to see the expression and joy on Billybobs and Flossie's faces. It was priceless!

A trip to the seaside always involves ice cream, and he loved that, too. Billybobs and Flossie were inseparable and only apart when one of them went to the groomers or vets.

We sadly only had Billybobs for fourteen months. Soon after we got back home, we had to visit the vet, as Billybobs had gone from our bouncy boy to a lethargic, very poorly boy in a matter of two hours. The vet said he needed an operation, but things were not looking good.

Sadly, Billybobs passed away under anaesthetic, and he never came home again. His intestines had burst and poisoned him. We were devastated and couldn't believe it had all happened so quickly. The fourteen months that Billybobs was in our lives were full of love, fun and joy. It was so worth it, and we think of him as we do all our rescues every single day. The rockery is now a permanent reminder and memorial to Billybobs.

Although devastated at the loss of Billybobs, we were determined to rescue another dog.

We didn't wait long before we were back at Immingham again.

Our latest rescue is Bear, now called Olly. Again, he was not the dog we went to look at initially, but after the last time with Billybobs, that didn't matter. When Kelly brought Olly out, I thought, what a handsome boy with his white chest and grey hairs on the end of his paws and tail.

Flossie took to him as he was quiet and reserved. Flossie, being our primary concern, had to like him for it to work. He was the last of a litter of dogs waiting for a forever home. He had never had a home and was two years old. I couldn't believe he was only two and had grey hair already, but his passport proved his age: not that it mattered.

Floss took to him straight away, so we went for a little walk with him to see what he was like. He was very nervous and wanted to go back in the direction of the kennels all the time. It is evident from his posture and all his movements that he was a very nervous, anxious, and frightened dog. He lacked confidence and was always looking over his shoulder, scared of all the noises and everything he hadn't seen before.

As there are only the two of us and we are both retired, we decided to take Olly on a foster basis to see how it would work out. Floss took to Olly very well, and he was good in the car on the way home but shaking all the time.

When we arrived home, he went to look around the garden and see his new surroundings. He was so frightened of everything and everyone: the washing machine, TV, vacuum cleaner, etc. We managed to calm him down, but we couldn't even open a packet of crisps without him running away. If you crossed your legs, he reacted like he would be kicked out of the way. We have never dealt with such a scared dog.

After a couple of days, he realised we would not hurt him and relaxed a little. We decided to keep him and give him his forever home. Getting Olly trained has been quite difficult as he has never had a home. We had the usual house-training issues, and he always chewed anything we gave him as a bed. We decided after a while perhaps it was the fleece-type fabric he liked to chew, so we let him sleep on the sofa in the conservatory.

Unfortunately, he chewed that too, and then the door-mats and a pair of my flip-flops. We sprinkled pepper on mats and the chewed part of the sofa, and that stopped him from returning to them. We bought a cage for him, but he was so scared of it that he wouldn't go in the room it was in. What to do now? We placed things on the sofa so he couldn't get on it, so I made another bed for him [now number three]. I used some material I had that was not fleecy, and we have never looked back from then on.

House training has been difficult with him never having a home before, but again, time, patience and lots of love have got us there. He sleeps in the conservatory as he will still not go upstairs, but he has settled on that, too, even though we don't like it and would rather have him upstairs with us.

He has a basket of toys he plays with all the time. At bedtime, all are taken into the conservatory with him, and he knows if there are any missing. When we get up in the morning, he takes the toys one by one into the lounge to be with him again. He is so gentle and has never snatched or taken Flossie's food.

He was very afraid when on his lead and hid behind me when we stopped to talk to people on our walks, his tail tucked between his legs and ears down in a submissive pose if anyone approached him. He was also scared of traffic. Time and lots of patience have got him to walk in a calm manner now, and he is much better.

We have had Olly for just over eight months now, and you would not believe he is the same dog. He gets excited and loves his walks, and we can let him run free in the local park, and he comes back and sits beside us. If he gets distracted and is going to 'take off', we just call him, and he returns. Anyone who knew

Olly before and saw him now would not believe the difference in him.

We can do absolutely anything with him and touch any part of his body with no reluctance. He tolerates a bath, goes to people on his own terms, and loves to play with us and his toys. He loves Flossie and likes to know where she is if she is not in sight. Flossie doesn't play much due to her age, as she is coming up to fourteen, but Olly loves her, and I am sure she loves him, too.

Our loving, friendly, happy boy has finally found his forever home. I don't think we have ever had a rescue dog with so many issues. With him being so timid, time, patience, love, and understanding have paid off.

This is our ninth rescue, and what a day it was when we discovered Immingham Dogs Home and met Kelly. Billybobs and Olly, as have all our rescues, have brought so much love and happiness to our lives.

Where would all these lovely dogs be without Kelly and all who help in the rescue centres? It is hard when you lose a beloved pet, but I always think they are with us. I love the fact that you have given another dog a forever home, and the love and happiness you gave to them are being passed on to another animal to enjoy being loved and cherished as they were. God bless them all.

Ella and Elsa

When we first saw a picture of Elsa, we were immediately captivated by her stunning beauty and the unmistakable depth of love radiating from her.

During our initial meeting with Elsa, my first impressions revolved around how timid she seemed, as well as the abundance of love she possessed and the extent of her kindness.

Her first reactions to us were timid and scared. When she was introduced to our two other dogs, Sadie, a Jack Russell cross King Charles, and Chewbacca, a Samoyed, she was initially slightly unsure. Eventually, she started interacting and playing with the Samoyed and greeting the little lady. It was heart-warming to see her enjoying herself and having fun.

The first few weeks were slow and steady, and settling in had its trials, but we worked on it, and she got better. She no longer gobbled down her food as if someone would take it away from her and got used to playing on grass without being scared of it. This was with a lot of help from the Samoyed.

We discovered early on that she loved walks and enjoyed

looking out the windows. She also loves riding in the car and having fun.

Now, what disasters occurred? Well, that is a question. We ended up with a destroyed crate and a washing machine with a chewed seal, and a neighbour complained about them being out in the garden. However, we have overcome those obstacles and have so much love for her.

Her personality has developed so much since we first met Elsa. She has grown from this timid, scared little German Shepherd into this full-of-life-loving, cuddly dog. She still shows signs of being scared, as if we will leave her, but then bounces back once we remind her that she is loved and we aren't going anywhere.

The bond between the dogs has evolved into a caring, loving, and playful relationship. Our relationship with Elsa has also deepened significantly. The love we share with her is immeasurable, and it's a testament to the rewarding journey of pet adoption.

Tammy and Mando, [Mimi]

Where to start? My husband and I both grew up with dogs since we were young. Last year, we decided that something was missing in our lives. Yep, it was a dog.

We decided to stop all international travel and focus on getting our dog. We saved up and were ready to look. We posted on the Hibaldstow notice board asking about rescue centres: Immingham Dogs Home came up a lot.

We filled in the application and were asked to take a video of the garden. We have one in the front and one in the back, both fenced in. We were also asked to send a video of our new addition's location in the house. Well, that was easy; we videoed the whole house.

We are both home all day, so the new addition would never be left alone. When we go out, she goes out.

So, we made an appointment to go to the rescue centre on February 18th, 2024. We wanted a small dog as we would be travelling with her.

We saw a few dogs, and then she bought out Mimi [now Mando]. My husband picked her up, and that was it. We both fell in love. It's hard to explain, but we knew she was the one. She's a four-year-old Corgi with a little Jack Russell in her face. We had arranged to come back and pick her up on Thursday 22nd; we left the shelter and went shopping for beds, toys, blankets, food, bowls, and everything we could think to make her feel welcome.

It felt like a lifetime to pick her up. We put a bed and blanket in the back of the car. My husband laid her down, and I sat next to her to comfort her.

Day one, and the poor little thing was so scared and timid. We let her walk around and do her thing. She did try to escape a few times, but we knew that could happen. We bathed her, and come bedtime [we had one bed in the living room and one in the bedroom], she came to bed and slept all night.

The next day, she had a little of her breakfast and wandered around the house. She wasn't really eating or drinking, which worried me, but I knew she would when she was ready. We took her for walks around the village; initially, she was timid, wanting to escape.

I took her out one day, and she escaped from her collar. I have never felt so scared in my life! I ran back home, and there she was, sitting at the front door. After that, we bought a harness she couldn't escape from, and she never has since.

That night, we decided to put her on our bed. It was up to her whether she wanted to stay there. Well, five months later, and she's still there.

The first few weeks were not easy. She was just so scared of everything, any noise that she heard. We noticed she did not like anyone standing behind her, especially when eating, and we had to go first when we went out. It was a learning curve, but remember, we did not know what she has been through and said that however long it takes, it is fine. We have all the time in the world.

Gradually, she became more comfortable and took over the house. We loved it. She was and still is very uncomfortable/timid around men and strangers. It sounds crazy, but as I said, you never know what she has been through. At first, my husband couldn't get close enough to put the lead on; she was completely attached to me and wouldn't leave my side, not even when I went to the toilet. As we both said, as long as she is close to one of us, it's better than none of us.

Sometimes, Mando gets biscuits in her bowl as a snack. She's so cute; she takes one biscuit into the living room, eats it, and then returns for another. It's too cute.

Moving forward, my husband can take her lead off, but she still won't get too close to him. But every night when she goes to bed, she curls up to my husband all night sometimes, right next to him on his pillow. She has come so far in a short time; she's spoiled rotten, and she's not just a dog. She's our child, and we love her death.

We have been to Blackpool, Liverpool and next month to London. She loves the hotels: Travelodge accept all dogs, which is brilliant. Last week, we went camping for the first time. She did amazingly, so proud of her. She never leaves our side and loves sitting in the garden in the sun. She also knows where to sit when we have food, right next to my husband. She now lies right by him on the sofa.

Every time we travel, we have to stop at a bakery. She loves her steak and bake.

She sleeps, and at every opportunity she gets, she goes upstairs to bed. We know she still has a long way to go, but every day, she does something to put a smile on our faces. When we visit Grandma, she jumps up on the bed and chills out. She also visits Grandad but doesn't get too close; she is definitely not as scared and timid as she was.

We take her to a car boot sale every Sunday as we try to get her used to people. She does great; if we go to a pub, whether inside or out, she always jumps onto the bench or chair and is so good that half the time, people don't even realise she's there. She's not a barker only if someone gets too close to her, but that's just her being protective. She wouldn't hurt a fly. She still has issues, but that's just time.

Every morning when she wakes up, she goes crazy on the bed, running around making funny noises and being silly; then we go downstairs, and I say, "Do you wanna go out?" Well, she runs around the living room and table for about 5 minutes, going crazy, then sits for me to put on her lead, and when she is back, my husband always has her breakfast ready for her, and she knows it: sometimes it's the little things in life.

We know she's happy and loving life. We have so many adventures to look forward to as a family. She had definitely filled the missing gap in our lives, and we wouldn't change a thing,

Even on her first vet visit, she was so good, even when she got her shots.

She loves car rides, has her space with her bed in the back and is so good even with her seatbelt on.

Stella, Mattie, Reuben and Charlotte

Hello, everyone. My name is Stella. I am the luckiest girl because I have everything I need. I have a warm bed, a cosy home, food and drink, treats, lots of walks, and visits to the playpark. But most of all, I have a mum, dad, and brother who love me very much.

However, it wasn't always that way.

I used to live many miles away in a place called Romania, and my life wasn't the best. Then somebody came along and helped me travel to a new country called England, where I was put into a home with lots of other dogs. It was all very scary, and I wasn't really sure about all the new things around me. I was very confused and didn't really mix well with the humans. Although they were all very kind and gentle, I preferred my own company or that of Mattie, who quickly became my best friend.

Mattie and I bonded over our experiences and everything I had been through; he had, too, so I found comfort in his presence. He made me feel that I wasn't alone and that I had someone to turn to when I was extra scared. Mattie was also nervous and didn't like loud noises, but whenever he got worried, one of the nice ladies at the home stroked under his chin to soothe him. He really liked that, and it helped him a lot. Sometimes, I was led into a field to meet new people, but this wasn't something I enjoyed as I felt everyone was looking at me, and I didn't know how to behave. What made it worse still was that Mattie wasn't with me. I just kept my distance and ran around. I was soon put back in with Mattie, much to my relief.

This all changed one warm day in June 2023. I was taken once again to the field and met a young couple. They tried to talk to me, but I was my usual shy self, and I just did what I had always done at times like this and then waited to go back to Mattie. But today was different, and the young couple took my lead. I looked over to where Mattie would be waiting for me; pulling to see my best friend again, I trotted happily on. But they walked me past the gate and put me in their car. I was totally confused and utterly devastated. *I can't do this alone,* I thought as they strapped me in the back seat. The young lady sat with me; they both spoke very gently, and I felt that they were nice people, but I just didn't know them, and this isn't what usually happened after my visit to the field. It was a long journey, and I wondered what Mattie would be thinking right now; I hoped he didn't think I had chosen to leave him.

When we finally stopped, I worried what was going to happen. Everything smelled differently, and I couldn't hear the familiar barks of all the other dogs I had grown accustomed to hearing. The young man carried me from the car as my legs didn't seem to want to work. He put me down in a strange room that I didn't recognise, but I found comfort in the corner of a rug, and that is where I stayed. I didn't like to move and found it hard to look the young couple in the eye. The young man carried me in and out of the house a lot so that I could go to the bathroom. That first night in my new home, I hunkered down in the dark corner of the garden, not sure what was expected of me. I was soon carried in to sleep on my soft, warm rug.

I started to go outside on my own more often. But I still could not relax and hid behind a chair I found in the garden if anyone came to visit. I felt very alone even though the couple were very loving towards me.

I was so scared; this was all so new to me. I didn't know what a home was, and having someone to myself was something I had never had before. My humans fed me and kept me safe, and they let me do my own thing until I started to get a little more confident. They were very patient with me. I soon realised I could trust them to look after me and looked at them as my mum and dad.

I didn't like leaving the house, so my dad often carried me, putting me down to walk a little, but as soon as I saw a bush, I would pull to go under it and lay down and hide. Poor dad had to carry me home some days - I think I wore him out! Then we started jogging around together, and walkies became more fun. We explored the neighbourhood, and I got to know and add to the scents on the grass verges, lampposts and gutters near our house.

I began to really love my mum and dad and knew that I was safe with them around, but something was missing. I still didn't feel complete, and I longed for that little dog that had kept me company throughout the whole journey, Mattie, my best friend. I worried about him and where he was and wondered if he ever thought about me, too. Well, I didn't have to worry for long. It turns out my humans had also been thinking about Mattie! They knew I missed him, and when they heard he had been returned to the home because he was also missing me, they jumped at the chance to let him come live with us. They were very sneaky, though; they didn't tell me what was happening.

One day, Dad took me to the back garden ... I looked, I sniffed, it couldn't be, could it? ... yes, it was my best friend! We started to play straight away as though the last four weeks apart had never happened. So it was; Mattie officially became my brother forever.

Mum and Dad often tell us how happy they are they have us, and Mum often cries happy tears at the silly things that we do [Dad has 'big manly' tears, too, at times, but I pretend not to notice]. You see, Dad had always wanted a dog of his own, having been the big brother to Pippin, Matilda and our Uncle Roland over the years. Mum had Scrappy, who was her best friend as she grew up, and so she too missed having the pitter-patter of tippy-tappy toes around the place. Dad works from home and used to spend the whole day talking to our brother James [the corn snake] when Mum wasn't home. But James doesn't answer back and certainly doesn't want to cuddle or go for walks. So, it was the ideal time to start looking for that doggo to make their house a home.

Dad told us he looked and looked and saw many wonderful faces on the homes' website. Then he saw mine. He instantly fell in love and showed Mum, who also thought I was beautiful. It certainly makes me feel special that out of all my wonderful friends, they picked me.

They wanted to meet me straight away and were so excited. When we met in the field for the first time, they didn't let my shyness put them off and understood that I needed time to flourish. So, when Kelly asked if they wanted me, they did not hesitate to say yes. I am so pleased now that they did.

As I said at the beginning, I have everything I could ask for and more. I love my life, and although I am still a little cautious of new people and experiences, I am easily won over and couldn't be happier. Mattie still jumps a little when a strange noise goes off, but he sees and feels his family around him and soon realises he's okay.

We love going on walkies and get so excited when Mum and Dad get the harnesses and leads out of the cupboard. I spring in the air, and all my paws leave the floor at the same time. Apparently, I remind them of a little goat, whatever that is. The humans think we don't understand when they spell W A L K I E S ... but we really do!

They take us to the playpark to mix with lots of other dogs in a big field. It's great fun, and I run around meeting all the old and new faces. Sometimes, we meet up with other Romanian doggos, and Mattie and I enjoy sharing our experiences with them as we trot around the field. I'm so happy, and I have a big smile on my face as I gallop around with my 'arms and legs everywhere' as my mum and dad always say. Mattie thinks it's ok and plods stoically around the field, taking his time, and prefers to introduce himself to the humans, particularly if they are giving out treats ... Mattie loves treats. In fact, Mattie just loves food full stop and sleep and finds great comfort in them both, which is ok as long as he watches his waistline!

Mum and Dad say I enjoy judging people. I guess it has something to do with the look on my face at times. I just think I was born that way and can't really help it if whoever I'm looking at feels judged. I feel very protective in a motherly way towards my family and often look at them with love in my eyes - when I'm not judging them, that is. I think it's great that when Dad pats his chest, I put my arms up on his shoulders as I'm nearly as tall as him. Mattie tried it once, but he decided that was too much effort. So, he just taps his front feet when he wants attention, stretches out, stares and smiles his usual wide smile until he gets it. I, too, have learned to stretch out my long arms and wave my paw for fusses. It really works! Dad says we're just funny kids.

Grandma and Grandad Chicken [so-called because they bring us specially cooked chicken as a treat and not because they have wings and cluck] come to visit us, and they give us big fusses, and we give them big kisses back. Funny to think we used to bark at them and hide when we first met them a year ago. Sometimes Auntie Chicken comes to stay with us if Mum and Dad have to stay out late. It doesn't happen often, but it's fun when it does. We lay there, and she gently brushes us with her hairbrush ... it's so relaxing!

I can safely say our family loves us, and we love them too. I am so happy Mum and Dad picked me from the pages of faces that day and then also brought my brother home to live with us. We are living our best lives and are forever grateful.

* * *

My name is Mattie; I'm Stella's brother. I will be forever thankful to whoever brought me over from Romania, as I live a wonderful life with my sister, mum and dad.

I don't say much as I'm the quiet one who thinks a lot, the one who plods through life eating and sleeping. Well yes, I do like to do that, but my life has not always been so easy, and I've not always looked so content.

When I came to England, it was confusing but good, as all of a sudden, I had lots of friendly faces around me and no shortage of meals; I certainly wasn't going hungry. But the best thing about my journey was meeting my sister Stella. We looked out for each other; she was a constant source of comfort to me. If I was anxious, especially if there were any loud noises, Stella would be by my side, and if I looked at her beautiful, kind face, everything would be instantly okay.

That is until one day, Stella went for a walk without me, something that she had done before, so I wasn't overly worried.

However, she didn't come back that day. I waited and waited; I looked around for her, sniffed the air for her familiar scent ... nothing! I didn't understand. I really hoped she was okay, but surely she wouldn't choose to leave me. We were a team! I missed her so much, and life wasn't as much fun without her around. Now my best friend had gone who knows where I became more withdrawn and preferred my own company. I just wasn't myself, and on returning home from visiting a nice lady's house for a week, I think people realised I was missing Stella far too much.

When I met my new mum and dad, I didn't know that they had the biggest and best surprise in store for me. After being taken into a special room, I was introduced briefly to the young couple, who I first thought were there just to give me nice treats, but then they took me for a ride in their car, and I thought maybe it was my turn to stay with them for a week, so I sat stoically in the back. They seemed like a caring couple and spoke softly to me and joined me in their conversation as we drove along which was nice. Then Mum took me into a garden, and we sat down and waited ... I didn't know what for ... but I didn't make a fuss. Then all of a sudden, I could smell something ... a smell I knew all too well ... Stella! We played and jumped around; life was good again. It turns out, somehow, Mum and Dad knew we both needed each other so that we could continue this adventure together.

Now I have my special place on the sofa where I like to relax and eat my treats; Mum and Dad even bought me a special headrest that they keep telling me are steps to help me climb up to my special place. I don't know about that, but it makes a great place to lay my head once I have leapt over them! Resting my head is a priority of mine, and I love snoozing with my head propped on any pillow, anywhere. Sleeping is a fantastic pastime, don't you think?

Along with my hobbies of sleeping and eating, I like to do a bit of gardening. In fact, I have made some super holes in the garden and love to lie proudly next to them, wondering what else Mum and Dad could possibly fill them with other than the mound of soil I piled up next to them.

I love it when Mum and Dad take Stella and me to the play-park, which is a nice day out. I tend to leave the main socialising with our fellow doggos to my giddy sister while I schmoose the humans. I particularly like those who are generous with the treats. I plod around with them and pretend to take great interest in their conversation, listening intently and then, in recognition of my polite manner, they usually hand over the sweet treats ... bonus! Apparently, I have perfected the widest smiles, which always goes down well with the humans.

I sit like a good boy when Grandma and Grandad Chicken come to visit, and I thoroughly deserve all the fresh-cooked chicken that they share with my sister and me. I enjoy the cuddles and fusses that I get now just for being me. I no longer jump when my back gets touched [I really can't remember why I did this]; now, it's just another place to be tickled.

I love my life, I love my family, and I know I don't perhaps say it enough, but I am one very lucky doggo.

Sharon, Copper, Rosie and Casper

My niece and grand-niece would walk their dogs with me and mine up along the beach every Saturday morning. I had Casper, a King Charles Spaniel, who was thirteen, nearly fourteen at the time, and Rosie, a Labrador.

Rachael and Alyssa had been volunteering at the dog shelter for some years, and when we were hit with heat waves in June and July 2023, they were unable to go volunteering in the afternoon when the sun was too hot. So, a few different Immingham dogs would accompany us on our early morning walks.

Copper had come along several times and was so happy and well-behaved; even though he was a little shy, he seemed not bothered by any of our dogs. At first, he was reticent to human touch, and sudden movements would make him flinch. I knew he had been at the shelter for a while and had no real interest in adopting him.

I offered to foster him, and after a week, he accepted my partner, too. He then slowly started to come out of his shell. Rosie and Coppy enjoy playing together and with toys.

He has been living with us for over a year now and has settled in well. He's much more comfortable with human affection, too. Sadly, we lost Casper recently at the grand age of fifteen. Having Coppy has made this loss easier for Rosie, who had spent most of her life with him. Coppy loves his morning walks at Weelsby Woods and has now started accompanying me to the allotment for more adventures.

Alyssa, Dylan and Eric

Our rescue journey started after my husband and I discussed getting another dog. We already had a three-year-old Cockapoo called Winnie, who was our little fur baby and my best friend. We knew that if we were to get another dog, we wanted to rescue given the number of puppies bought and surrendered during lockdown. So, we went in search of another Cockapoo to join our family.

We applied for several dogs; however, we were rejected each time because the dogs would go to my parents' house while we were working. We started to feel really disheartened by the process. Then I came across a picture of Eric, a three-year-old Cockapoo who had had two previous homes. I immediately told my husband, "I have a weird feeling we're going to get him, you know." Well, that feeling was right, and before we knew it, we were having a home check and on our way up to Immingham with Winnie to meet Eric.

I remember Kelly saying, "He's not a bad dog; he's just been really misunderstood," so we went into the meeting with very open minds. Into the pen came Eric, a scraggy-looking Cockapoo who was more interested in investigating the smells in the pen than entertaining us or Winnie. Despite this, we knew he just needed time and patience to truly come out of his shell, and we felt like he was our dog, so we bundled him into our car and brought him home.

The journey home was interesting; Eric started off in the backseat but didn't want to sit with Winnie, so he pushed his way through to sit on my knee in the passenger seat, a brief glimpse of his affectionate side.

Once home, things were running smoothly; Eric let us bathe him and settled relatively well into his new surroundings. Little did we know the tests that Eric had in store for us to make sure we were the right humans for him.

For several months, we had no cushions on our sofa; Eric stole and guarded anything he could get his paws on and destroyed any toy we bought him. Eric ate anything and everything in sight, whether edible or not, which led to multiple vet trips. We soon discovered that Eric despises the vets as well as having his hair cut! Eric would chase anything that moved quickly, including joggers, birds and cyclists; he growled at anyone he wasn't sure about and people standing up/approaching too fast.

After several months of this, we felt we didn't understand what Eric needed and began to doubt whether we'd made the right decision for him. So, we enlisted the help of a dog behaviourist who helped us understand where the behaviour was coming from and helped us improve Eric's behaviour. Eric's personality is now totally different from the one we initially brought home; for the first time in his life, he feels safe enough to show his true self.

Eric is a big teddy bear. He loves to be loved and close, and he makes the perfect bodyguard. Once he trusts you, he'll do anything for you and let you do anything for him, which is probably for the best, as we're his personal groomers, ear trimmers, and nail clippers.

A family member who's had dogs all of their life often says, 'I've never met a dog more ADHD than Eric', which sums up just how boisterous his true personality is. A dog that's so nimble he can vault over the kitchen island better than an Olympic gymnast whilst simultaneously being so clumsy he runs into the patio windows regularly. A dog that one minute can be staring into your soul with his beautiful big eyes, batting his long dark eyelashes at you, and the next be giving you side-eye.

Due to his dopey nature, we weren't sure if Eric was actually a Cockapoo, so we did a DNA test to get some answers, although we were sure we loved him either way. From the test, we found that Eric is 39% Poodle, 26% Cocker Spaniel, 25% American Cocker Spaniel, 2% English Springer Spaniel, 2% Field Spaniel, 2% Welsh Springer Spaniel, 2% Miniature American Shepard, 1% Portuguese Water Dog and 1% Lagotto Romagnolo. So it turns out the majority of him is indeed Cockapoo, just a truly bonkers one who doesn't quite have the intelligence of his big sister, but we love him all the same.

We've now had Eric for nearly two years, and his bond with Winnie has become really close; he is very affectionate towards her despite her keeping him in his place. We've had some hiccups along the way with Eric's health, and after lots of visits to see Brian, the vet [Eric's arch nemesis], we now know Eric has some allergies which cause health problems. Luckily, Eric's love of food has enabled us to put him on a minimal-ingredient diet, which seems to be doing the trick.

When Eric was initially advertised, he could not go to a home with children due to incidents in his previous home. With Eric making such huge improvements in the rest of his behaviour, we also had several successful interactions with children. Eric is now so calm and loving around children that he brings his ball for a one-year-old family member to throw and lets him pat his head and ears. In fact, he's come on so well that on a recent holiday in Wales, a young child approached Eric and wrapped his arms around him. Eric took it like a champ despite us internally bracing ourselves for an adverse reaction.

Moments like these make us incredibly proud and make us realise just how far he's come. Eric has made a huge impact on the whole family, and being able to interact with different family members has made him much more trusting of new people. It's amazing to see Eric thriving and being his fun-loving self. We're all just glad that he is truly happy and so incredibly loved.

Jeanette and Freya

Hi, I'm Jeanette, and I adopted Freya in February 2023.

I picked her up from her foster home in Doncaster, and she came straight to me and jumped in the car.

When we got home, my grandson had to pick her up as she wouldn't go in the front door. She had a good look around the garden and then explored inside. She found her new bed and loved it immediately.

We had a few days where she wouldn't go through doors, but as she gained confidence, she managed it. Her safe space was beside my bed, which she often visited in the first few weeks.

We had a few problems with her food, but after visiting the vet, she's on low-fat gastrointestinal food. She's a bit overweight, so we try to keep treats for bedtime. She loves apples, carrots, and other fresh fruits throughout the day.

She's a really loving dog and always goes where I go. I don't drive, so she only goes on walks near home. She's not keen on other dogs, so she's not allowed off-lead.

I was feeling down, so I wanted a dog, and I think she fits

the bill, even when she jumps about wanting her meals. We complement each other quite well.

Aimee-Lea, Mishu and Rosa

Where do I begin with Mishu?

I never saw myself with another dog in the near future. But one day, on my way back from a family event, I was scrolling Facebook, not even looking for a dog, when this scruffy, curly-haired ball of fluff caught my attention, and I just knew.

I never believed in love at first sight, but I knew the moment I saw his picture that he was my boy, no matter what it took. But I was nervous. Having two children, one of whom was only one year old at the time, I prayed we would be suitable for him.

I nervously rang Kelly to ask the question as his advert said he was nervous and quite scared. She was happy for us to go and see him. We agreed it would be without the children first, as we wanted to see how he took to me on my own.

A few hours passed from the initial phone call, and I was sent the details of his foster home. I agreed to meet him that day on a walk so that it was all on his terms; I remember sitting in the car park just waiting for him, and then he appeared. My mind was made up. I felt more in love with him. I didn't think it was possible.

On this walk we went: he kept his distance at first, and I chatted to his foster mum about all she had learned about him and what I could do to make him feel comfortable with me. By the end of the walk, he was coming closer to me.

Fast-forward a few days. I had the home check, and it all felt very real. It was time to take the children with me, and it went perfectly. My eldest needed a bit of work, understanding that he was nervous, but after that, all three of them got along fine, as my youngest kept his distance at first. So Mishu loved that; after all, he was nervous, too.

Then came the day: Gotcha day. I was so nervous about bringing him home, so I made sure I went alone to get him. He let me pick him up and put him in the car, and I knew from that second that it would be okay, as he had allowed me to pick him up. The rest was history. Honestly, he hasn't left my side since that day.

Two weeks later, I braved a dog show with a nervous dog. You can imagine the sweaty palms. How would he react to the dogs? How would he do with all the new people? All that worry for nothing as he was such a good boy and came home with quite a few prizes from classes he won. He enjoyed seeing everyone from the kennels, especially Kelly, which is when I learnt Mishu's tragic backstory.

He was one out of eleven puppies found on the side of the road not more than a few days old and suffering from the dreaded parvo. While all the other puppies sadly passed, Mishu was the one who made it, and he braved the journey from Romania to the UK and stayed with Kelly and the team. They all fell in love with him for his cheeky personality when he let you in. We all believed it was because of his crazy coat, which is why I fell in love with him.

This dog show was also where I started my foster journey, which led to me helping seven other dogs, some of whose stories are also in the book. I also helped with a few adoptions. I began a wonderful friendship with Kelly and the team at the kennels and couldn't help but want to help.

The first few weeks were a breeze. I discovered Mishu was a big baby and adored his cuddles and personal contact. He much preferred his late-time walks when he could sniff to his heart's content without the risk of a nasty stranger being near him. Some people couldn't always understand why I advocated for him, and I made them aware to keep their distance as he would be scared of them, but I knew he trusted me, and I wouldn't let anyone hurt him. We also learnt he loved his crate for his personal space as sometimes the house could be overwhelming, which I completely get having a one-year-old child at the time: I sometimes wished I had a crate for some space!

I quickly learnt he loved all treats; his favourite is anything bacon-flavoured. He hated water and was terrified of it, but anything else being brushed or being groomed, he loved. He was the perfect first dog. He welcomed each of the foster dogs into his home and showed them all the luxuries they had to take advantage of since leaving the kennels. But after the seventh dog left, I noticed Mishu was starting to struggle without a playmate, and I made a very crazy decision, which led me to the next part of my story.

* * *

Now, whilst mine and Mishu's story was very much love at first sight, mine and Rosa's story was very different. Rosa has a very quirky way of greeting people. She jumps up at you and barks quite aggressively at some people, which puts them off her.

After going up to the kennels for about two months, I

finally met the diva that was Rosa. I went through the greeting and thought, 'jeez, this dog is crazy'. Gradually, every time I saw her, the barking got less and became more excited barks, so I thought, hmm, maybe.

I had heard she was Mishu's kennel mum and his roommate, and whilst she liked to be in charge, Mishu was happy to be bossed around, so they were the perfect pair. I sat and thought about the decision that was weighing on my mind. Rosa had lived in houses previously, one of them being with a lovely lady who had fallen poorly and had to give Rosa up due to not being able to give her the care she needed. The other home wasn't suitable for Rosa. It had made her very guarded, and I needed to be sure I could handle all her quirks.

At the time, she was being considered to be a sanctuary dog, which meant she wouldn't be up for rehoming again as her greeting put people off. But actually, when you got past that, she was so loving and caring, it was a like different dog.

What I also had to consider was taking her from a place she was so very comfortable at. She was so very loved at the kennels when she wasn't being a diva, and I knew it would be a big adjustment from that environment to my home. So, I worked on building up my experience with other rescue dogs and fosters before making my decision, which was agreed upon with Kelly. She would come to me as a foster to see how she settled.

The day of picking her up arrived. This girl jumped in the car as if it were her birthright and took her favourite spot in the car. Once I got her home, she had a good sniff around and said hi to everyone, and I quickly discovered she loved my grandma. For a dog who barked at everyone when she first met them, my grandma didn't get one bark. In fact, she lay at her feet and expected cuddles straight away. She was perfectly fine with both the children and was so excited to see Mishu.

After about an hour, I couldn't find her anywhere. Now, I

knew she had not gotten out because both doors were locked, so I hunted everywhere to try and find her. I discovered her in my son's bedroom in front of his cot, fast asleep. When I tried to move her, I quickly realised she was still very stubborn, and, in fact, she didn't move for three hours. I also learnt she is fiercely protective of the house and will put on her loudest bark at any noise to scare anything off.

I knew then she would never leave my house unless I was going on holiday and she needed boarding. I knew I was going to adopt her, and she was going to spend the rest of her days with me being loved.

She quickly took to living in our home, barring the odd toilet accident, but with a bit of patience, we sorted that. I quickly learnt that she prefers women over men as she tends to calm down with women much quicker. She loved her crate for personal space as she had used that at the kennels. Walks, I thought, would be my biggest problem as when she was at the kennels, she wouldn't walk very far. But after a few weeks, she was out walking with Mishu and loving their walks with all the new smells and sights.

I've learned many things in the nearly two years after being a doggy mum to two rescues. Mishu will forever be that big baby I brought home, and I wouldn't change him for the world. He's learnt that not all strangers are big and scary, but he still likes to bark at them. Water is still scary, and he hates bath time and will howl afterwards like his world has ended. He likes to provide Rosa with backup when she barks, even though we all know he wouldn't hurt a fly. Mishu gives the best hugs when he flops on you, and he loves to be cuddled. His favourite place to sleep is laid in my bed, tucked up under the quilt with his pillow just right. Or if I don't do his pillow just right, he has to have his paw touching me. He's very big on personal touch, and I don't mind that.

Rosa has learnt she doesn't have to bark at everything, but she thinks it's so much fun. She has learned to give paw for treats, which is amazing for her stubborn bum! She's learnt to love walks and will bark happily once her lead emerges. She's learnt Carter, my son, is her best friend when he has snacks as he will share with her, and her favourite spot when the nasty fireworks are going on is under Carter's bed as it's nice and dark and quiet under there. Her favourite place to sleep is in my daughter's bed with her, and even when my daughter isn't home, I catch her in there.

And to think this all over started over scrolling through Facebook and seeing a picture, and I gained two dogs who I wouldn't change for their world no matter how many times they bark and eat my tea.

These dogs saved me in a way I didn't know I needed saving, and I will be forever grateful for them both; they've helped me grow in so many ways on days when I didn't know what to do; they insisted on walks or cuddles. They've also both helped my daughter in so many ways. Rosa becomes her 'safe space' when she is feeling down. She will spend time cuddling her, which comforts me because I know that many moons ago, no one thought it would be this way for Rosa.

I am so glad I took the chance with her and Mishu; I really am. I am eternally grateful for my gorgeous dogs, but I am more grateful to Kelly for taking the chance on me and giving me the opportunity to love these two dogs more than I ever thought possible.

Lisa and Rufus

It was December 2022, and I had been without a dog for two years. I had decided to retire, and it was time for me to get another dog.

I decided I wanted a rescue Staffy and mentioned this to my friend Helen. She then sent me some pictures of Rufus.

I immediately fell in love and contacted Immingham Dogs Home regarding information about adopting Rufus. I spoke to Aimee-Lea, who explained everything to me. I sent videos of my gardens as requested, and everything was okay.

I went to meet Rufus, and he was absolutely adorable. I took him for a walk. He was excited and pulled a little bit on his lead, but when he settled, he walked so well, no pulling at all.

I had another four visits to take Rufus out, and every time I saw him, I loved him more and more.

I finished work on 28th January 2023, and on 29th January, I came to collect Rufus to give him his forever home.

Rufus wasn't cat-tested. I have an old cat, and Rufus and Jess got on so well together. I didn't know what to expect, as I had never had a rescue dog before; you hear so many different things. I was absolutely amazed at Rufus. Not once has he wee'd or poo'd in the house. He just goes to the back door.

Rufus has three best friends: Poppy and Thomas, the Pugs next door, and Gumball, the Yorkshire Terrier. They just play together, and it's lovely to see them. Rufus is a chatterbox. He literally chats with the human neighbours, and we swear he was sent to me by my partner and my other Staffy, who passed away. He loves lots of love, cuddles and walks.

We came to the Easter Show, and it was only a couple of months since I had Rufus. I entered him in the best rescue group, and he only went and won first prize; it was a very emotional mummy moment.

I am so blessed. I couldn't imagine life without Rufus. He really helped me through my depression and made me realise what a wonderful life I actually have.

A lady named Jenny saw my posts. She was one of the ladies who looked after Rufus before he came to Immingham. She said she was so happy Rufus had found a loving home, and I said it was the same with me finding Rufus.

I love him so much, and he knows it. The only thing is, I wish I had a king-size bed!

Jayne and Beau

Before I adopted Beau, we had a really tough year that had been full of loss. We had lost my cat Pudding to old age [sixteen], shortly followed by my dog Scooby to old age [fifteen], and if that wasn't bad enough, we also lost my dad and my two godparents.

All three of my children had been asking for another dog, but I kept putting it off. I know how attached they get and how much of a big commitment it is, but honestly, the house had never been the same without a dog being part of the family. Scooby was only a small dog, and he brought so much joy. I'd had him since birth, so my two eldest children had grown up with him. He helped them through so much as they were growing up; he was amazing, and it was a bond they greatly missed.

So, I started looking at rehoming kennels, as all my previous dogs had been rescue dogs, and they have all been fantastic. I happened to scroll past a picture of Beau, and I just knew I had to find out more about him. I sent a message and found out he was in a foster home just around the corner from where I lived, so after completing the home check, we went around to meet him.

On meeting him, he was just as beautiful as his picture. I'll always remember the size of his ears, which looked far too big for his head, but he had the most loving eyes, and we all instantly knew he was the one.

Beau was there lapping up all the fuss and belly rubs and treats his foster parent had given the kids to feed him, and he was so gentle with my four-year-old; I remember looking at my partner and saying, he is our new dog. I instantly fell in love with him, so the deposit was paid the next day.

We were all so excited once the time came to pick him up; I fetched him before the kids got home from school, so it was a nice surprise for them. The moment Beau came to his forever home, he sniffed around and then claimed his place on the sofa on a fluffy dressing gown with the teddy dog toy we bought him. He had a bit of a fuss and then fell asleep with his legs in the air. It was like he knew he was here to stay.

After a few days, he started to show his playful character. The only real issue I had with him was that he used to try to play-fight a lot, but after getting in touch with his foster family and getting their advice, he soon calmed down.

As we got to know him more and he got to know us, he has grown in confidence; it has taken a lot of hard work and finding the correct harness for his walks as he pulls like a freight train. It was like he couldn't get to where he was going quickly enough, and he thought everyone you passed down the street was coming to play with him. He also used to get excited when any litter flew past him and would try to start chasing it as he saw everything as something to play with. His character is so cheeky and funny; even today, if he sees a sock lying around, he will pinch it and turn it into a game of chase.

He is still unable to be let off his lead, so we take him to different fenced-in dog playfields so he can run off his lead. He just gets so excited and distracted by everything around him, so we are still working on his recall.

I can honestly say that adopting Beau was one of the best decisions I have made. He has such a funny personality and the affection he shows my kids, and they show him is amazing. He behaves completely differently with them all; it's like he has a favourite thing to do with each of them. He is really gentle with my youngest, and he loves going to see Nanna for treats and to see if he can pinch a slipper when she's not looking!

Life would certainly not be the same without him, and I would be lost without my shadow following me around wherever I go. With his cheeky personality, I'm looking forward to many years ahead. He has brought so much joy and smiles; I could not imagine life without him.

Kelly's Story

Those of us who have adopted from Immingham Dogs Home already know how much hard work Kelly and her team put into rescuing and rehoming dogs. So, for those who don't know, here's a little insight into Kelly's world!

How long have you owned Immingham Dogs Home?

Immingham Dogs Home started as Immingham Boarding Kennels and Rehoming six years ago. I initially boarded dogs for other rescues and helped the rescuers. After our first local dog show, I realised how much support we had locally and made a huge decision to rescue myself and become a charity. That took over a year of filling in forms and going back and forth with the charity commission, but finally, in October 2023, we got our charity status.

Why did you choose to own a rescue?

I don't think anyone chooses to own a rescue, but I started fostering for Amicii Dog Rescue eleven years ago. That turned into me being more involved and becoming head of rehoming and a trustee. From there, it was just something I had a huge passion for, and, as well as making a difference, I enjoyed it.

What did you do before?

Before I made the crazy decision to move to Immingham and work with dogs full time, I worked in a primary school teaching. While I was still working, I had been fostering many dogs over those years. I learnt so much, so although it was a huge jump from kids to dogs, it wasn't just a snap decision.

How many dogs do you have yourself?

I have five dogs living in the house: three I have officially adopted and two long-term fosters. Ruby, Arthur, and Buddy are officially adopted. Hayley and Broomie both foster me, but they will never leave, as they all have needs or issues that made us decide to keep them here.

How many dogs do you have at any one time?

We usually have up to 40 dogs, but we frequently have a list of dogs waiting to be rehomed, and this number has increased even more in the last few years.

We have eight dogs living here permanently who would find it difficult in a home. Then we have eleven others that are very difficult to rehome as they need a specific type of home. All are happy here while they wait, and we love them all.

Do you have patrons who support you?

We don't have a patron as such; we have many people who support us regularly. We have a 'fairy dog father' who helps us massively when things get really tough, but he prefers to remain anonymous.

How many people volunteer at Immingham Dogs Home?

Our volunteers fluctuate a lot in terms of walking the dogs. We have about twelve regular people that come rain or shine on certain days of the week. Then we have others who come now and again to help when they are able to. We then have our volunteers who do the home checks; we have six people who do these, and we couldn't rehome without them. Then we have

Olivia & Jade, who do all the paperwork for adoptions, email payments, etc. Once they have done that, Sally will change the microchips, and Shelly will do the follow-ups. We have Shakira & Shelly help with the Facebook page, Shakira runs the Instagram, and Leah runs the TikTok. All on a voluntary basis.

What are the major challenges?

Vet bills are a big challenge, as so many dogs come into us not vaccinated or spayed. Making sure we always have enough food is a massive one. We have a regular donator for a lot of our dry food but not tins or treats, so we are always running out. Paying general bills - people forget we have to pay for the water, electricity and all the general running costs of a normal physical building place. Currently, the biggest challenge with the dogs is getting the larger dogs into homes. Small dogs come and go, but bigger dogs go unnoticed; it's been like this for around twelve months now.

What does a typical day in the life of the home look like?

A day at kennels

5.30 am - get up, let my own dogs out, make coffee and get ready.

6.30 am - outside to get food ready.

7 am - start feeding and cleaning kennels - other volunteers and day staff start at 7.30 am.

8.30 am - start walking the dogs - we usually do around 5/6 walks each, depending on the number of volunteers.

10.30 am - finish walking - check all the kennels are still clean and the dogs are all ok.

Everyone usually goes home at this time. I use this time to groom dogs, fix things, do paperwork, and answer the many messages on Facebook and phone people.

1 pm - go and check on all the dogs again - clean any kennels that need cleaning.

1.30 pm - we start walking the dogs again.

4.30 pm - feed all the dogs and clean any kennels.

5-6.30 pm - nearly every day, this is usually a vet trip of some kind.

6.30 - 8 pm - let dogs out in the gardens for a quick wee break before bed, give them all a bedtime treat, and put them all to bed for the night.

What is the relationship with Amicii?

Eleven years ago, I offered to foster a dog I had seen on Facebook for Amicii. From there, I became a trustee and head of rehoming and rehomed many Amicii dogs. We have some of their dogs here long term as they have been returned over the years; although I left Amicii four years ago as a trustee, I still have a strong connection with many of the dogs and people, and if I can help, then I will. Especially as I helped rehome many of them. My two long-term fosters are Amicii dogs. I am not involved with their current rehoming or adoptions, but I'm still in close contact with many team members.

www.imminghamdogshome.org

www.facebook.com/imminghamdogshome

Registered Charity Number 1204865.

Eleanor, David, Serena & Aled

Serena

Age one and a half approx.

Serena was initially found as a stray puppy, around five-ish months old, living next to a motorway in Romania. She was taken home by a very kind older woman but could not go inside the house because her dogs would not take kindly to Serena; this continued for a while. The woman fed and loved her, but neighbours did not like Serena hanging around. A wonderful woman took Serena home, fostered her, and loved her as her own for around a year until she arrived at Immingham Dogs Home. They took her into the kennels and took such amazing care of her, as they do with all the dogs, and I met Serena there.

I had been volunteering at Immingham Dogs Home for a few months and discussed possibly adopting a dog with my partner, David. We agreed to try, provided the dog accepted our three cats and vice versa. It was a risk, but one I was desperate for as I fell in love with so many dogs at the dog's home [inevitable, really!], and I wanted to adopt one to give all my love and time to. I wanted to bring one of them into our little family. We waited a few more months while we were buying and moving into our first house, and then it seemed the perfect time to try it.

I asked Kelly for a dog for a sleepover to test the waters to see how the cats are with a dog and if it was indeed feasible. The dog I asked for, Lilly, was not cat-friendly; therefore, Kelly offered Serena. I recall walking into the kennels, and a dog called Bob came running over. We had a good cuddle and a laugh, and then I saw Serena's tail wagging nervously but excitedly. She was panting with nervousness. She was a beautiful ginger colour, almost fox-like. Small and fluffy, she was beautiful and so sweet.

She came slowly over and offered her head for a love. I remember thinking there and then, yes, this would work. I wasn't worried or nervous myself anymore. I loved her instantly; I felt she was my dog at that moment. Crazy, really. She was so sweet, leaning gently against me for a cuddle. I sat on the kennel floor with her, and she put her head into the crook of my neck and gave me the sweetest cuddle.

She was nervous walking past the other dogs, so I carried her. She met her daddy, David, and she went straight to him and put her paws up on him. She leaned her head against his leg, asking for love. David said, 'She's quite sweet, actually, isn't she?' He was originally more nervous than I was about bringing a dog home. We felt she loved us from the start, too, as Serena doesn't tend to like men.

She is now much more confident and accepting of men being near her and accepting of strokes, but for the first few months, she was very scared of men but loved David from the start. She is a daddy's girl, always sitting on his knee or curled up in his lap, held like a baby!

We took her home; it was like she had always lived there. She didn't mind the cats and didn't chase or bark at them. She loved the sofa and the bed; mostly, she loved a cuddle, wanting to be as close as possible on your knee or curled up against your side for belly rubs. She loved walking too, smelling everything and walking super-fast, with her ears back, head down, tail up, pulling, and chasing anything small and furry when outside.

Sadly, however, we had only asked for a sleepover, and come Sunday, when we asked to adopt Serena, Immingham Dogs Home told us she was already reserved by someone else and was being adopted the next day. I spent all of Sunday clock-watching, dreading 4 pm and the time to take her back. It broke our hearts to take her back, put her in the kennel, and then walk away; I cried the whole car ride home.

By some miracle, on Monday, the person who was adopting Serena came to the kennels to meet and pick her up. Serena was not interested in them and did not want a cuddle. She walked away from them very nervous and fearful, not at all sweet and fussy like she was with us. She did not want to be stoked or fussed. That person adopted a different dog, and I got a text to come pick my dog up when I could.

I was at work and cried when I read the message [twice in two days!]. I never usually cry at all. Straight after work, I went to pick Serena up. I was not even going to collect any essentials; I was more worried about the person who was going to adopt her changing their mind.

Serena was super excited to see me. She came straight over and asked to be picked up, whining and kissing me. We had sat on the sofa in the kennel reception for a while, where she started to fall asleep on me as if to say thank goodness you're back. I knew you wouldn't forget me; I can sleep now. It was like she knew I was there to take her back home, which we did after I returned to collect my car keys. I was so focused on Serena that I had left the keys behind! I think that's why she didn't want to go with the other person; she had already found her home and her mum and dad.

Serena settled into our home amazingly well. She took it all in her stride, house-trained, slept through the night, and was great with the cats. A few times in the first few weeks we had her, if we were both at work, which wasn't often, she would use the cat's litter tray to poo in! Something she doesn't do now, almost a year later, especially as she has a canine brother; she can't have him thinking she is a cat!

Serena slept on the bed the first night at home. I remember turning the light off and stroking her, and she had a little growl. She wasn't used to the dark and having people so close to her. So many things, like the kettle, air fryer, and cans opening, used to scare her. She soon learned they were okay and took it all in her stride. The stairs confused her for a while, and watching her go up or down them was hilarious for the first week.

On walks, she was very nervous. She wasn't used to or didn't like the lead and used to try to run or twist to get free, but it didn't take long. After around three weeks, walks became much easier, and she learnt they were not so scary and could be fun and filled with squirrels. David and I, in turn, learned dogs could apparently climb trees; she can get higher than you think up a suitably low branch tree or bent tree. I have had to take my shoes off and climb up after her to get her down from a tree before.

Serena also learned how much she loves toys. After a few months, she became more confident and started playing. A corner of the living room is now called the 'toy corner' where she keeps all her stuffed and squeaky toys; if we put them away, she gets them back out one by one and puts them where they should be in the toy corner.

Serena is the pickiest eater. She doesn't really like dog food. In the early days of adopting, Serena would refuse meals for days, so we took her to the vet. After that, we tried many different brands of quality dog food. Luckily, we recently tried her with raw dog food, and she loved it.

We bought another new freezer just for the raw dog food. Pampered princess, much! She's done really well since; her not eating for days was the only worry we have had with Serena, but she loves raw food and raw treats! Possibly, it was due to her starting as a stray, eating road kill. We think this may be the reason, but we will never know for sure.

Serena is the sweetest girl and such a happy, playful girl. She is the best thing that ever happened to us; I really do feel we were meant to be, we were meant to meet, and she was meant to be a part of our family; I think she feels the same. Dogs have incredible resilience, loyalty, and the capability to love and forgive. Serena would have every reason to hate people, abandoned on the motorway as a puppy, left to fend for herself for survival, and yet she was the sweetest, most gentle, loving girl; dogs really are amazing.

Aled

Age four and a half approx.

In 2021, Aled was found as a stray in Romania; dog catchers had caught him as he had been attacked by bigger dogs and had an injured back right leg, which slowed him down and meant he struggled to walk. He still limps today, though it causes him no pain or suffering now, thankfully. He was taken to a crowded shelter in Romania where amazingly kind people sponsored and cared for him, and he was eventually sponsored to come to Immingham Dog's Home in 2024. It was there that I met him whilst volunteering to walk the dogs.

I met Aled the very day he arrived, in the play garden at Immingham Dog's Home. He and the three other dogs all looked like our dog Serena, a ginger corgi crossbreed with fluffy knickers and little legs. Kieva and Pip, the other dogs, looked the spitting image of Serena; Aled is a little bit bigger and is a darker ginger.

They were all lovely dogs, but it was Aled who I felt such a connection with. He drew most of my attention. It was him who I gave the most cuddles and chicken pieces to. I recall walking him for the first time as a volunteer. His limp gets worse when he's nervous or if he's walked too much. He was very nervous about everything, from the new environment to the people. To help him settle, we walked just down the street, sat on the grass, and cuddled. He loved the long grass, and he turned a few times, then lay down where he made a makeshift little grass bed and gave me his belly and paw. Sweet and gentle right from the start, he just wanted love.

I remember the next time I visited him in the kennel, the other three dogs were really enthusiastic about being fussed, and Aled was sitting with his head bent against the door, looking like he wasn't bothered about love but kind of like he had given up. I stroked his chest, and he straight away pawed at me gently for more and slowly came over, secretly desperate for more love.

Each weekend that I walked dogs, I went into Aled's kennel to fuss and spend time with him. Every time, I loathed leaving him. Weeks later, I asked my partner, David, to agree to a sleep-over to see how Aled was with cats and how Serena would be with another dog.

We picked Aled up with Serena straight after work on a Friday night; David agreed he saw how much he looked like our Serena, a large part of the reason why I fell in love with him so quickly; all Serena's fault! Aled was initially nervous, but after walking around the block, he forgot his nerves enough to walk next to Serena and David.

We initially kept Aled apart from the cats for the first few hours to let him smell them, and they him. He enjoyed solo cuddles in the kitchen and many treats as he's massively food-driven; he is the opposite of Serena in that he will eat anything. After a few hours, we let Aled have the whole house. Initially, he was very scared of the cats, whining or barking so we could move the cat out of his way so he could pass, something he still does now. He never chases or goes for them; however, he's an amazingly sweet boy, and we got very lucky with choosing him.

Aled slept in the kitchen for the first week to give him time on his own to decompress and settle in. I would pat his bed, and he would lay for a tummy rub and kisses before tucking him in under a blanket and with a few treats on the floor for midnight snacks. In the morning, he would give the biggest tail wag and present his stomach for a rub; it was the highlight of our morning!

Now, Aled sleeps on our bed between us, or he sleeps on the dog bed on the bedroom floor. As soon as he sees one of us is awake, he jumps on the bed and spoons one of us for a snuggle with a big wagging tail; he gives the best hugs. He lays fully on you and keeps you super warm even in heat waves!

He gets really goofy and excited when you call him or fuss him. He bends his head sidewards, leans, falls against you, whines, nibbles at our tops or trousers, and gives kisses on our faces. Giant goofball! Aled is not fussed about toys yet; even now, he just wants to be stoked, talk sweet nothings, and have treats, of course.

In the first week of adopting Aled, he leaned on Serena, his new 'sister', a lot about what to do and how to feel safe. He would get excited and tippy-toe from side to side, wag his tail and lick her face or really anywhere he could reach whenever she got up in the morning. If she went out and came back in, he wouldn't go on walks or into the garden without her. He loves his sister.

Unfortunately, after only a week of adopting Aled, we were

attacked by two off-lead dogs while walking, which we had no room to escape from. Serena was bitten, but luckily, only a small graze on her inner thigh. The person who owned the dog was gesturing and shouting, scaring Aled and causing the most long-lasting damage to him emotionally. Both Serena and Aled were traumatised for the next 24 hours. They wouldn't eat at all and ran around the house panting, constantly running to and from the window and door, convinced the dogs had somehow followed us home.

We stopped walking them for about the next ten days and focused on making them both feel safe and loved. Since then, Aled has been even more nervous of people and dogs; he is now terrified of strangers. Sadly, he gets scared enough to try to run and get away anytime people walk his way.

We have to cross the road often. But he has made a lot of progress since then, and he is back to enjoying walks. I feel he will continue to become more confident and be able to walk past strangers and maybe one day meet and happily let strangers stroke him again. We go to dog classes at Quality Canines, which greatly helps his and Serena's confidence. Serena has returned to her usual confidence on walks; we hope Aled will be there one day, too. He's been through a lot, and he's doing amazingly well.

Aled's favourite thing is being off the lead at the beach, away from people and dogs. He runs and gives doggy smiles; his floppy ears blow upwards in the wind. He also loves watching our pet rabbits in the garden. He barks and wags his tail like crazy. Aled is also very clever. He knows 'cross' means cross the street, 'outdoor wee' for garden time, and the word 'walkies', for which he gets very excited. He also understands hand gestures. If I point and say that way, he goes that way. So clever!

My favourite thing about Aled is when he nibbles and kisses you, always careful to do it on your clothes so he doesn't hurt you; so sweet! David's favourite thing about Aled is his ears, and how much they flop and how expressive they are; he always looks an inch away from taking off like dumbo. Aled also loves a car ride. He looks out the window, making sure to stretch to look outside every window and take it all in. Aled is such a sweet boy. He gives the best bedtime cuddles; he even shares the bed with my cats, Archie and Serena, too. Aled also loves a blanket. He cocoons himself into it, digging the blanket into a ball around him, then flopping into it, and will use the whole bedsheet if given a chance. He is a real blanket hog; it is a talent, really!

Aled has come so far from being a stray who was attacked by bigger dogs, crippled, injured and alone. From being caught by dog catchers and kept in a high-kill shelter where kind people did all they could to care for him. To being loved and cared for by Immingham Dogs Home, who worked so hard to build up his confidence, which led to his forever home with us.

Serena and Aled have changed our lives so much; they've made our lives infinitely better; they are a reason to get dressed and spend time outside and to remember to enjoy life a bit more and be out exploring, as well as to do nothing and chill at home. Whether we are on a walk around the neighbourhood, the woods or the beach, or having a cuddle on the sofa or playing, they are the best part of any day for me and my partner David. They are why we get so excited to come home and why we forget any troubles of the day, for the heroes welcome when we get home.

Serenas wagging 'helicopter' tail, and Aled's crazy tappy-toes and kisses from them both. They don't care why we left; they only care that we came home with such pure, unconditional love. They're the best. I wish more people adopted a dog instead of buying from a breeder; rescue is the best breed. They all deserve a loving home and a family. All dogs deserve a good life free from suffering.

Adopting a dog really does save a life. It allows real rescuers like Immingham Dogs Home to save the next stray, the next abused, neglected, starved, injured, unwanted, unloved, and abandoned dog. They'll be the lucky ones to be rescued and find their family and place to call home.

Sue and Sissi

The first time I saw a picture of Sissi on the Immingham Dogs Home Facebook page, I thought she looked cute, but they all do! I just saw a dog who needed a loving home and wanted to find out more about her.

When I first met Sissi at the rescue, it was apparent she was a very nervous dog. However, she did take a treat when offered and let me stroke her. I knew I had to give her the chance to have a loving home.

The first few weeks weren't easy. She was pacing around a lot, and I even didn't think it was going to work out. Then, bit by bit, she gradually started trusting me and relaxing a little.

She loves ripping up paper, including the bills, so I fitted a letterbox cage to catch the mail. It was hilarious when I went shopping for the cage. I said my dog is chewing my mail. I need a cage and they thought it was a dog cage. I said, 'No, one for the letterbox'!

She also loves digging the garden up, but again, that's a doggy thing. My previous dog loved a spot of digging!

Her personality developed very slowly. I'd say it took a good few weeks to settle in, and nearly a year later, she is still finding herself. She didn't even bark until around eight weeks after we got her.

She's a very loving dog. She loves me to fuss her, especially with an ear rub. She soon became very attached to me.

Our relationship has grown a lot in the year. She'll always be a very nervous dog, but in Sissi's terms, she's a lot more confident and feels she can be herself. She's learned a lot of words and phrases. Her favourite phrase is 'Would you like...'

Rex, Maverick, Alfie and Luna

When considering adopting a dog, it's important to reflect on your circumstances and past experiences. Have you had a dog before? Are you looking for a companion for an existing pet? These are questions worth pondering before taking the plunge.

We had a wonderful Labradoodle named Teddy, whom I hand-reared from two weeks old. He was an extraordinary dog, beloved by our entire family. Sadly, Teddy developed a tumour, and despite our best efforts with medication, his health declined. At twelve years old, we faced the heart-wrenching decision to let him go, prioritising his comfort over our own feelings.

Over the years, Teddy had become especially attached to my daughter, following her everywhere and always sleeping in her room. After he passed away, our home felt unbearably empty. We left his beds in their usual places in the lounge and bedroom, and every time I came home, I'd instinctively call out for Teddy, only to feel my heart break all over again. The silence in the house without him was deafening. Despite this, I was adamant that we wouldn't get another dog for a while. My daughter and I did share an English Setter named Jasper with my parents, whom we both adored, which helped fill the void somewhat.

Even though I kept saying I wasn't ready for another dog, I found myself browsing rescue websites. My daughter also kept tagging me in posts about two nine-month-old Labrador-German Shepherd mix puppies, a brother and sister. Curiosity got the better of me, and I inquired about the one that wasn't reserved, the male. I completed the paperwork, and after a successful home check, we went to the rescue centre with Jasper to meet the puppy.

We named him Maverick. From the moment we saw him, we were smitten by his cute, energetic nature. He had more Labrador traits than German Shepherd, and we decided to bring him home. Maverick's joy was contagious, and we couldn't help but smile the entire drive back.

Adjusting to life with Maverick was an adventure. We quickly remembered that young, large dogs require a lot of exercise, and those long walks in January weren't always pleasant! We started focusing on his socialisation, including weekly daycare visits, which were both fun and essential for his development.

A few days after bringing Maverick home, the rescue centre called to confirm his gender, as his supposed sister had turned out to be a boy. The family who adopted him returned him after just fifteen minutes. My heart went out to him. After discussing it with my partner, Chris, we decided to adopt Maverick's brother, who we named Alfie.

So, instead of one new dog, we ended up with two! Our lives were suddenly filled with chaos, laughter, and training sessions. The boys had very different personalities despite being siblings. Alfie, with a personality more like a German Shepherd but the appearance of a Labrador, would bark at any sound or visitor but was a gentle giant at heart. Maverick, who had more of a German Shepherd look but acted like a Labrador, had a habit of stealing shoes, slippers, and toilet rolls.

With our two boys and Jasper visiting frequently, our home felt full and happy. We thought our little family was complete - until we learned that Jasper's sister, Luna, needed a new home. I couldn't bear the thought of her in a shelter, so I inquired about her. After a meet-and-greet with the boys, where they all played and zoomed around the garden, it was clear that Luna belonged with us.

And just like that, our "no more dogs" rule went out the window, and we welcomed Luna into our home. Now, we have three dogs full-time, plus Jasper for occasional visits. I must be crazy! But with my flexible work-from-home schedule and enough space, it's all worth it.

Life with the three dogs is still in its early stages, but the boys have taken to Luna wonderfully, and it feels like she's always been a part of our family. Every day is filled with laughter and joy, even when things get a bit chaotic. Alfie, who's afraid of water, watches in disbelief as Maverick dives headfirst into any puddle or body of water he finds; he even attempts to hop into the hot tub while it is filling! Meanwhile, Luna brings her own charm and energy, making our family feel even more complete.

These past nine months have flown by. It's hard to believe how quickly our family has grown and how deeply our lives have been enriched by Maverick, Alfie, and now Luna. I may never have a clean and tidy house again, but that's a small price to pay for the love and companionship of our furry friends. Our home is full of doggy love, and I wouldn't have it any other way.

But please, don't show me another rescue dog, or I just might become the neighbourhood's official crazy dog lady!

Carole and Alice [Missy]

Tony and I moved up to North Lincs from Cambridgeshire just over three years ago, bringing with us one dog, Jay, a five-year-old border Collie x Lurcher, and two ponies. Our new large garden was already dog-proof, which was a bonus, and we soon started thinking about getting Jay a playmate.

We did look initially at rescues, but one centre needed us to get a family member to agree to take on the dog if anything happened to us due to our great age [over 60!]. Another needed us to fence off a small portion of our garden with six-foot fences to keep the rescue in until it got used to us. So, we decided to get a puppy and welcomed Florence, a nine-week-old Sprollie [a Springer/Collie cross], into our little family.

But, the idea of a rescue stayed with us. I joined a couple of local Facebook groups and saw Missy on the Immingham Dogs Home page one day.

A deaf and partially sighted border collie, about 12 months old: I showed her profile to Tony, something I had done every now and again when a dog had caught my eye. He didn't really say anything at the time, but as he went to bed that night, he turned back to me and said, 'If you would like to apply for that dog, then do'. I needed no further encouragement and applied then and there on my phone.

The next morning, I found a message sent at 6 am from a lady called Jade, making sure I was aware of the adoption process and asking for proof of identity and address, as well as a video showing the house and garden. So, at 7.30 am, I found myself making a mini video. Jay and Florence helped, running up the garden with me. That evening, I had a phone conversation with Jade and another one with Kelly the following day, and we arranged to meet Missy the next day [Saturday].

Saturday dawned, chucking it down with rain relentlessly. Tony and I had already agreed that we wouldn't make a decision immediately but that we would meet Missy and then go away and talk it over. Due to the weather, we met her inside; she was smaller than we expected and quite, quite adorable. Our sensible intentions went straight out of the window, and by the time we left, it was arranged that Kelly would bring Missy to meet our two on the following Monday.

Thankfully, Monday was a nice day, so we met in the garden. Jay and Florence were very excited to have another dog on their territory, and Missy was more interested in racing around and pulling up tufts of grass while looking up over her left shoulder. It was agreed that we would collect her the next morning.

Day one was interesting. Missy, now called Alice, ignored the other dogs and dog toys entirely; she just focused on any random object, patted at it with her front paws, and then ran away, looking over her left shoulder again and again and again. Jay and Florence were rather scared of her and kept very close to either Tony or myself. On the upside, and to my great surprise, she was clean in the house. She was also eating and drinking well.

She was keen to go for a little walk although nervous about cars, which we had been warned about. We put her in Florence's crate that night, much to Florence's chagrin as we had never put it away from Florence's puppy days as she loved it so much, although this was the first night the door had been shut for about two years.

We didn't hear a sound from Alice all night, and she was pleased to see us the next morning. Over the next few days, she started to settle with the others, although the obsessive behaviour continued. She also introduced barking into her little routine. We moved the items she focused on out of the way and distracted her with a ball. Florence's favourite became Alice's favourite, too.

We are now one month into our journey. These days, Alice and Florence play together like a pair of puppies, and Alice and Jay have races down the garden. She still exhibits some herding behaviour, Florence doesn't seem to notice, and Jay doesn't care; he is not to be herded! Thankfully, the obsessive behaviour is on the wane, and the walks are now a little longer, although she still doesn't much like moving cars. The crate is still there, but the door is left open; sometimes Alice sleeps in there, and sometimes Florence does. We hardly even notice that she is deaf now; sign language is king! And she still is quite, quite adorable!

Holly and Ted

Our rescue journey started at the end of 2023 when I chose to use my volunteering day at work to help at Immingham Dogs Home. I came away so impressed and touched by the kindness of the team there that the whole family came with me for a morning after Christmas to help walk the dogs. We couldn't help but feel a little guilty that we purchased a puppy three years ago rather than choosing a rescue, especially after seeing Immingham's amazing work and the wonderful dogs that find themselves there looking for a home.

From that moment, we had committed to finding a new addition to the family through Kelly and the team. We kept watching and waiting patiently. We nearly adopted a different dog, but the foster family decided they could not bear to part with him, so the wait continued.

Then, on the 1st of March, our patience paid off.

Ted appeared on the Immingham Dogs Home page. There were lots of comments on the post already. Being a "cute fluffy Cockapoo", we didn't think we would stand a chance with so much interest, and if we were honest, we never intended on another Cockapoo. We already had a three-year-old Mini Cockapoo [Wilson] full of attitude and energy in equal measure, and adding another crazy Cockapoo to the house wasn't really on our agenda.

We set aside our reservations and applied, and in a whirlwind of ten hours, we were accepted, home-checked, and a meet and greet arranged. Kelly warned us that he didn't quite look like his photo anymore as he had to be shaved due to excessive matting [if you had seen his photo, he looked like your typical poster boy Cockapoo; how could he end up in rescue?] We had no idea what to expect, but we didn't care; we'd made mistakes at the start with our own Cockapoo's grooming [we previously had an Akita for eleven years, so this had been a huge change for us at the time]. We had ourselves had to have our own cockapoo shaved quite short while we got used to the grooming.

The day we had waited for was finally here; we packed Wilson and the family into the car and headed to Immingham. When we saw him for the first time, we knew instantly he was the one; he walked in wearing a little stripey jumper to keep him warm and was so friendly and trusting. He loved Wilson [although initially, I am not sure the feeling was mutual], but Wilson soon warmed up. He was bald in places and had very little left of his beautiful coat; he was a little thin, but all things we knew we could sort out. We headed off on a little walk to see how they got on, and that was it: Ted was coming home with us.

I am not going to lie. The first few weeks were hard. We had prepared ourselves that it would be hard, but it was harder. The boys didn't settle well to start with, and play fights were becoming more than playing. Ted was mouthing, trying for dominance, and was quite reactive on walks towards other dogs. All things we were not expecting of a dog that was four, who, although he had clearly not had all his needs met, had not been abused or mistreated; at times, we felt totally out of our depth.

We reached out to Kelly at one point as we didn't know what to try next. She suggested we have a chat with Natalie at Quality Canines, and we quickly put some things in place with the dog walker and trainer we already used. We felt incredibly lucky that we already had some amazing people in our corner whom we had met when we got our first Cockapoo. Claire at Little Tinkers gave us perspective, support, and kindness, and without her help, we would have definitely gone mad trying to settle Ted. Erica at Paw & Co. chilled us out and supported us so much through socialising with Ted. To anyone struggling in the early days, the best advice is to reach out and get support. As the saying goes, a problem shared is a problem halved.

Things started to settle down gradually. We were getting more confident about dealing with issues, and it felt like we were beginning to emerge from the storm. Then, something happened that made everything make sense.

Ted's chip came back confirming we had, in fact, not taken on a four-year-old cockapoo as the owners had stated to Immingham Dog Home, but that he was actually only eighteen months old. Pieces of the puzzle started to come together. We had been here before with similar behaviours with our first cockapoo at the same age. The relief that we were not going crazy and that our instincts that something wasn't quite right were correct gave us another boost. We now felt like we knew what we were doing, that we were not failing Ted, and most importantly, we were giving him the home he deserved!

We had signed Ted up for Puppy classes at our trainer's advice before we found out his actual age, as he had no training and no social skills; we were starting at zero! Some weeks of training were tough, and I certainly left feeling slightly deflated occasionally. In others, we saw glimpses of the fantastic dog he could become.

By week six, he was graduating, and even in those six weeks, we could see how far he had come. What meant more was that the other people on the course also commented on how far he had come in that time and how well he had handled being surrounded by much younger dogs.

Next, we had Ted's first proper groom. Given that he had been very matted and previously shaved, we were a little worried about how he would behave, but he was a dream. He looked at the clippers and dryer and settled immediately after he'd checked them out himself. Visually, it was the first time it became obvious how much we had physically transformed Ted.

The biggest test for Ted was still yet to come, though. We had two short breaks booked before we adopted Ted, and both dogs were coming with us. It was as much of a test for us as it was for Ted. It turns out you need to pack as much for two dogs as you do for a newborn baby!

Ted took both holidays in his stride. He was brilliant in the car and settled really quickly into his temporary homes. He had a day in Whitby, which was extremely crowded, and there were lots of dogs in close quarters. He politely greeted those dogs he was allowed to, sat perfectly in the pub for a pit stop, and was just genuinely a total star. He put his brother Wilson to shame.

We are three months in now, and things still aren't perfect, but perfection is overrated. Ted is still a work in progress and probably will be for a little while yet, but the progress he has made is remarkable, and we feel very lucky that we were the adopters chosen by Immingham Dogs Home to join him on his journey.

Jenny, Phil and Little Mo

In October 2022, we had to make the heartbreaking decision to have our rescue Staffy, 'Eli', put to sleep. He had kidney failure and dementia; he became very ill during the night, and we had to meet our vet at the surgery at 05:30 on a Friday morning. Eli left a huge empty gap in our hearts and home.

We agreed we would not have another dog. He was my fourth dog and Phil's first. We both struggled with losing him. We decided to support a local dogs home and chose Immingham after reading an appeal for help on their Facebook page. We took Eli's leftover food, treats, and bedding to the home and donated to vet bills and food requests.

We would see photos of dogs needing homes, and then we saw Little Mo. A nervous-looking little fellow who resembled a Corgi crossed with a German shepherd.

We thought, 'Cute little thing', then 'Should we'?

We arranged to meet Mo, and although he was obviously timid, I fell for this little dog. Although we knew he was so different from Eli, gaining his trust would be hard work. The only thing we knew about his background was that he came from Romania in a litter of six puppies. All of his siblings have short legs and long bodies, but there the similarities end as they have different-coloured and length coats.

We passed the inspection after making sure that our garden was dog-safe. Things moved quickly, and we collected Mo on 17th March 2023. He was so afraid he spent the first two days and nights huddled up to the back door.

We had to be very patient, as he would only drink at night. He would also only eat if we didn't watch him. He would take small amounts of food and sit in a corner to eat. I believe he may have been the underdog in his Romanian kennels. Even when he is travel-sick, he does it silently. It's almost as if he doesn't want to draw attention to himself.

On the third day, we saw his little black-masked face peer around the living room door. He suddenly cleared the width of the room and landed on the sofa next to me.

Mo slept next to our bed, and after a loud bang outside, he decided to jump on the bed and has slept with us ever since. He mainly sleeps on his back with his legs in the air. He dreams almost every night, making loud yipping noises and running in his sleep.

After the first week, we took him to our static caravan on the East Lincolnshire coast. I stayed for five days on my own with him as my husband was at work. Mo instantly loved it there, taking long walks on the Saltmarsh. He showed us what a magnificent tail he had, carrying it like a feathered flag where he had kept it tucked under his body before.

He showed fear around people, especially children, bikes, pushchairs and anything noisy. He would spin around and hide in the grass as far away as his lead would allow. Now, he sits just out of reach of the people we talk to.

He didn't play with toys until he stayed at the caravan. He

prefers cloth toys, dismantling them and leaving a trail of stuffing until there is very little left.

After spending most of the summer and autumn at the coast, he gradually became braver and more confident. However, he also showed his stubborn side by sitting down and refusing to move if he didn't like where his walk was, which Kelly at Immingham Dogs Home has noticed.

Mo returns to Immingham for his holidays, which he enjoys as he plays with other dogs.

Over the winter at home, he has made some dog friends on our regular walks. However, he is still very wary of people and only lets one other dog walker touch him. He is very gentle, so I can groom him, cut his nails, trim his Grinch feet, and bathe him without problems.

Mo likes to visit my sister's caravan [which is on the same site]. He will bark at her when she visits ours but sits quietly there; he has a friend in Kobi, her elderly Newfoundland: a strange but cute sight, this little and large pair.

Over winter, we introduced Mo to a safe dog play compound. He enjoyed running and sniffing, but on his third visit, he decided he didn't want to come home. He proceeded to spend the next forty-five minutes over his allotted time running away from us. It was bitterly cold and frosty. I was getting worried and upset, imagining us there all night in the cold and Mo being frightened. Anyway, we finally caught him with the help of a dog owner and his two very boisterous dogs. Mo now visits there on a long training line.

We Googled photos of Mo and believe he may have Kokoni in him. This is a Greek breed known for making a lot of noise. They were bred to warn Farmers' wives of intruders. He certainly tells us when there are strangers about.

Little Mo hasn't replaced Eli and never could. We are pleased we decided to get him, as without him, there would be an empty space in our lives. We have to get up to walk him, which makes us appreciate early mornings and nature.

We continue to support Immingham Dogs Home by donating to their dog food account and, when possible, towards vet fees.

Kelly has been great at offering support when we thought Mo would never wag his tail for us, which he now does daily. He makes us laugh at his hopeless attempts at catching flies, watching his zoomies on our Saltmarsh walks and digging in the sand for the elusive sand monster.

As I write this last paragraph, he is doing his guard dog impression at the window. Oh, and did I say he has 'Dobby' ears when he does this?

Shakira

Kelly's daughter is an integral part of rescue life; here's how her days pan out.

What is your role at the kennels?

I work within the rescue in many ways. Daily, I walk the dogs along with our volunteer walkers. We all spend quality time with them and love them. This also includes cleaning their kennels, feeding them, and, of course, spoiling them with their bedtime treats when we tuck them into bed at night!

I also run our Instagram page, which is a daily responsibility as I try to constantly update our Instagram followers with pictures of our pooches to make people smile! Another daily job I do is responding to Facebook messages and the kennel's texts and calls. Alongside my daily jobs, I also organise all the dog shows.

We usually do three a year Easter, Summer and Christmas. Each one involves different planning, as we try to cater each event for each season. For example, we contact Santa to visit our Christmas show [we all know how busy he is at that time of year!] and the Easter Bunny for our Easter show!

Planning the events takes a lot of time, as I have to ensure I advertise a good few months before and arrange and organise stall holders. I plan all the different fundraising we will do at our shows to raise money for the dog's home. At past events, we have raised a good amount of money; at our most recent summer one, we raised a huge amount of £1416.47. We couldn't pull off such amazing shows without the amazing support of the community attending and helping us raise funds!

I also deal with the sponsorships we have for our dogs while they stay here. Sponsoring a dog involves setting up a standing order monthly, with an amount of the person's choice. We then give back by setting up a sponsor chat and sending regular updates about the dog which they have chosen to sponsor whilst staying with us.

The sponsor money goes towards paying for the dogs' needs while they stay with us, such as their food, vet bills, and treats [we go through treats quicker than ....]. However, we don't overfeed them; we just spoil them, as they deserve!

Why did you become involved?

I became involved in the charity when Mum started it. I wanted to help out, and I'm glad I did, as I absolutely love being here.

Do you get much downtime?

I get a small bit of downtime, which always includes travelling, as I love seeing new places! But any other downtime I do manage to get, I spend with my own dogs, taking them out on new walks and seeing new places or planning events for the dogs' home.

Do you own your own dogs?

Mum and I share the dogs we have, as I live with Kelly [Mum] here, so yes, of course, we own our own dogs! We have five in total, two of which are mine, Ruby and Broomie. I have had dogs in my life since I was a baby, so I've always had a love for dogs, and I treat my own like they're my children!

Do you ever feel sad when a dog leaves?

We all get attached to the dogs here; we love each one of them like our own! So sometimes, when they find their forever home, it upsets us, but we always know they will be just as spoilt in their new home. It can be much harder when the ones who have been with us for a much longer period of time leave, as we have created such a special bond with them after spending such a long time with them. As much as it makes us sad, we are also extremely happy for them to find their happy ending.

We all play so many roles in the daily care of the dogs that it's difficult to list them all. But showing them off on social media certainly helps people become aware of us and our actions. It also makes people smile, following a rescued dog through to being adopted. On our rescuers page, seeing how the dogs develop once they have left us is lovely. Their confidence grows, their personalities develop, and they are loved and become the centre of families. It's often the case that the dogs rescue the new owner, too!

Please contact Shakira at Immingham Dogs Home if anyone wants to sponsor a dog, requires information about events or would like information on volunteering at the Dogs Home.

Jess and Didicus

Here's how Didicus adopted me!

I wasn't supposed to be getting a dog. I'd not long lost my beautiful Pomeranian, Troy, and was chatting with my partner about moving in with him and his cantankerous Boxer, Tank.

I really missed Troy's wagging welcome and ever-judgmental presence, but I was strong. That was until my sister sent me a post from Immingham Dogs Home. As soon as I saw those big bat ears, I was smitten!

I tried to tell myself no, but I kept thinking about his sweet little face, so I messaged. I explained that I was working full time, telling myself they would rule me out, but that was fine. I asked how he was with other dogs, thinking I would again be ruled out, but no, he would be happy with a friend! So, I applied!

I had a video home check, and to my relief, I was accepted. Before I knew it, I was on a road trip to Cleethorpes to meet 'Diego'! My friend accompanied me in case he found the car ride challenging, and we stopped on the way to buy him some essentials, including a stuffy.

I was nervous on the way in case he didn't take to me, as I believe that they choose us more than we choose them! I didn't need to worry; as soon as the door opened, I was greeted by a little black piglet all excited with the new people. Then we gave him the toy, and he was no longer interested in anyone!

Following a reassuring conversation with lots of tips and advice, it was decided Diego liked me well enough to give it a go. So, we were on our way home. With no hesitation in coming with me, he jumped straight in the car and made himself comfortable. There was not a peep out of him the whole way home. We made a little pit stop in Louth for a toilet break [for all of us], where he met his new gran, and then all the way to Boston without a whimper.

Once we reached home, I opened the door and said, 'Welcome home, little one'; with that, he was straight in and exploring. He had no fear and was looking in every corner, but he kept checking in with me to make sure I was still there. I had the chance to have a good look at the weird little gremlin who was running around and into everything. There were his big bat ears, his underbite, a snaggle tooth and some kind of lightning bolt that I assumed was his tail. At that point, I decided that he wasn't really a Diego, so I researched the name and came across its Latin version, Didicus. I knew instantly that he was a Didicus, and he seemed to approve.

That first evening and night, I was worried my new friend wouldn't settle, but there was no need; he treated it as home straight away, and when I asked him where he wanted to sleep, he was like, 'The bed silly'*!* And so I had a new bedfellow. Secretly, I was thrilled until the snoring started!

We spent the first week getting to know each other. We went to get his collar and tag and some much-needed toys, which he promptly dismembered. I'm still traumatised by the legless, wingless flamingo. Didicus met his new Dad and his great-grandparents, who were smitten from the first second. For a funny-looking bat dog, he was stealing hearts wherever he went.

Someone who wasn't as easily won over was Tank. Dids wanted to sniff and play, but Tank wasn't quite so sure. This was the real test, as their relationship would determine the course of mine. After several weeks of gentle introductions and a lot of growling, and the time Tank banged his paw on the sofa and bounced Dids right off, Tank started to come around begrudgingly. He took the hint that this noisy little piglet with no respect for personal space was staying. And so they now enjoy the normal sibling relationship of squabbling and jealousy! But there are moments when they forget the pretence and show they love each other with cuddles and play. And yes, we managed to move in together as one hairy family.

I have been so lucky with Didicus. He settled in straight away and took everything in his stride. We learned he likes to sleep within a 'leg nest', all curled up with me and helps develop my contortionism skills! He likes his meals like a toddler, with his biscuits, meat, and fresh food in separate piles and not touching each other, all served on his Disney Stitch plate! It is also obvious that he wants to be a lizard, with his tongue spending very little time in his mouth. You have to be quick not to get a dog snog, but he is often faster!

I hope Dids has learned that he is safe and loved by me and so many. Despite me telling him off when he's yelling at the neighbours!

Didicus is such a gentle soul who has helped fill a Troy-shaped hole in my life. He is an entirely different dog, which is not a bad thing. He still exhibits some diva behaviour that would make Troy proud, like having to sleep on all the pillows!

I love all the cuddles; he has so many to give. I love our games, and I love his comforting presence.

Thank you, Immingham Dogs Home, for giving me the greatest gift. It's been nearly two very happy years, and I look forward to many more, giving Didicus the opportunity to live his best life.

Joanne and Sophie

My previous rescue dog had a 'V' shaped bald patch on her back where someone had burnt her with an iron. She passed away in 2019 with kidney failure; she had also gone blind.

I've had rescue dogs all my life, and I was lucky to get Sophie in March 2020. As I cared full time for my mum, having a dog to walk was my 'breath of air'.

I wasn't aware of Sophie's story when I adopted her from Kelly. But after my interview over the phone with Varda, I was invited to meet Sophie on the Saturday. I met Kelly, who advised me to go into the bungalow grounds to meet Sophie without any distractions, as she was a 'nervous dog'.

Kelly brought Sophie in with a bag of treats and said that once she trusts you, you will be fine. Kelly thought she was around six months old. Sophie was black and white, short-haired, and on the small side. She was frightened when brought to meet me and didn't want to leave Kelly's side. I just saw this beautiful black-and-white face that needed some love. I spent a good while with her, trying to reassure her. I really was unsure.

I wanted to be the right person for her. She was so scared of everything.

I wanted to help her and wanted the best for her. I talked with Kelly about my concerns, and she said, 'It's your choice, but she will be OK with one-to-one'.

So, I decided to help Sophie. I took her home to Scunthorpe. She got out of the car and into the house. I showed her her bed and her toys, and that was it. She just lay on her bed shaking. After an hour, I tried taking her out; she was so scared of everything. I kept talking to her from a distance, but she wouldn't move. I showed her water and food, but she wasn't interested, and I didn't want to push her.

I wanted her to relax and come on her terms, but I knew this would take time.

I tried taking her for a little walk every two hours, but every noise was scary. Eventually, after ten days, I managed to get her into the playing field, and she seemed to perk up when she met other dogs.

My neighbour had just got a puppy cockapoo, Izzy, and I used to walk Izzy when he was at work. I had an idea. Would meeting Izzy give Sophie some confidence?

I decided to take Sophie and Izzy onto the field together, and bingo! It was like Izzy said to Sophie, 'It's OK; she gives nice walks, lovely treats, and is friendly.' They were soon racing around the field, chasing each other; it was a joy to see! I filmed it and sent it to Kelly to update her on Sophie's progress.

I was surprised when I got a video from Daniel in Romania. He was the one who had initially rescued Sophie and said it was good to see her happy. I watched the video and cried. Daniel was in a field chasing a horse and cart! On the back of the cart, you can see a white sack of bricks and Sophie's head hanging out with wires attached! The next stop was the river. Thank

God Daniel was there. But it did impact upon me, and I could now understand Sophie's mistrust of people.

Sophie is still a nervous dog, but she trusts me now and used to love my mum, who sadly passed away in January at the age of 91.

Mum taught Sophie some bad habits, like giving her some toast at breakfast with Lurpak butter; thankfully, she's not having that now. She used to sit by my mum's chair because if Mum had a biscuit, she would share it with Sophie.

Now it's just Sophie and me, and I think we have rescued each other. When I'm down and missing Mum, she seems to know and brings me a squeaky toy to play with.

Even now, a year on, Sophie goes to check my mum's bedroom as she did when Mum was here. She likes to patrol at night. She lets me lock up and put the lights out, waiting for me to be in bed before she comes upstairs and checks Mum's room before coming into my room, where her other bed is. She has a bed in the lounge, too!

It is a work in progress with Sophie. She loves her walks, especially when she can chase her friends in the field. But she is still very wary of people, but I'm hoping that will cease in time.

Sophie, Dan & Zac

I first saw Zac while volunteering. I loved his kind eyes and scruffy fur straight away.

Considering his injuries, I was surprised to see how well he walked and moved. He had been involved in a road traffic accident, and his spine was fractured between his femoral and sciatic nerve, so some of his leg muscles didn't work. I loved how much he loved life and people despite what someone had done to him.

He was the most loving dog we had ever met. Every week, I volunteered and saw him there. Ann had fostered him, but she travels a lot with the rescue, so he returned to Kelly [Immingham Dogs Home]. He had his own room and was out with Kelly most days, and he chose which dog he wanted to sleep with each night: he had a pretty good life.

Dan first saw Zac when I brought him home for us to foster for a long weekend. He was very cute in a scruffy way and showed great determination in walking, especially as vets thought he would never walk again. But he defied the odds and worked out his own way.

Back at the Dogs Home, I spent more time walking and fussing with him, and I just couldn't wait to see him every time. Dan knew he was going to be a 'foster fail' and stay at ours more permanently.

When we first had Zac, he wanted fuss and cuddles and was very excited: maybe too excited! He cuddles you like a human, putting both of his paws around you. He's an old man at heart and likes lots of rest.

Zac has an extreme love for cheese, which we share too. We found that he had a habit of spinning around in circles when he was happy. He absolutely loves car rides, journeys, and just being in the car seat, even if we aren't leaving the house. He has an equal love for sitting on office chairs and sofas, just like a human does.

At first, we had all the small accidents you can imagine with having an incontinent dog until we got his nappy routine sorted and dealt with yeast infections and other nappy-related issues. We found that Aldi size six nappies fit him best out of all the other brands, including ones specifically designed for dogs.

His feet are always vulnerable and at high risk of infection. This had been a battle for Kelly as Zac managed to get to his infected foot, turning a minor issue into a large one. But thanks to Kelly and myself caring for him, we avoided him having to have his leg amputated, and he started to heal again. Full recovery may take up to six months.

While on a walk, Zac decided a deer would make a good friend and followed them. He finally came home when he was satisfied he could not find them!

After a year of being near each other, he developed a lovely bond with our house rabbits, Cinnamon and Comet. They nose-boop Zac from time to time. He enjoys sitting and watching them like it's his own live TV stream. He does tell

Comet off if he chooses to run to the front room instead of being in their home in the kitchen.

He loves his routines, including having a special breakfast of scrambled eggs and sausage on weekends. He can now tell us when he wants his nappy changed by giving a particular bark and comes happily to the room where we change him. He stands and waits until he is changed, then will go once his new nappy is on. He will also lie down, let you change his bandages, and wash his back feet.

He also likes visiting places where he will be fussed by many, like garden centres. He loves meeting new humans and has been to different festivals and country fairs with us (folk music), and he enjoys going camping and being in a tent. He also enjoys his holidays and loves the long car journey to France!

Whilst away, he sprinted off across the beach, sat by the sea and waited for us to catch up with him while he sat and stared across the water. Zac doesn't like swimming; when the water touches his chin, he goes into panic mode. So we acquired a shark dog life-jacket to help, which he very reluctantly wears for a paddle.

It took some time for us to adjust and develop a consistent routine for Zac due to him being incontinent and needing extra care with his hind feet (bandaging, cleaning them) and wearing boots. Once we learned how to develop a care routine, Zac was much more settled and so were we. It wasn't an easy adjustment for any of us, but we wanted the best for him. His love for humans and his cuddly and loving nature made these times much easier for all of us.

It took Zac a couple of years to feel entirely safe with us and realise that he no longer needed to protect us against other people coming by the house.

We needed to find a way for Zac to get around easier, as it was affecting his mental health. So, a local charity is making him a set of wheels so that he can zoom around to his heart's content.

He's grown to know when we are feeling sad or poorly and will happily give us a cuddle or sit near us to check we are okay. He truly is a toddler in spirit and heart, and we love his zest for life!

Judith and Poppy

About 40 years ago I had my first rescue dog. At that time I was living in Birmingham and Sola, a collie cross, came to me from Barnes Hill, RSPCA. She chose me and as her time was nearly up I had to adopt her. She meant so much to me that when I lost her I was really broken up and felt I could never have a dog again. I adopted a kitten who grew into a beautiful and special cat but I eventually lost her to uncontrolled epilepsy.

I also have an adopted son with complex special needs who came to me from London. As he was in and out of hospital for extended periods as a child a friend looked after Sola for me some of the time. As my son's needs were so great that was another reason I could not adopt another dog.

I have been on my own now for some time now, I am retired, in my seventies, my son lives nearby and visits regularly. Last year, as I felt very much alone, I started looking for a smallish dog who would fit my current situation. I was looking at different rescue organisations for about a year until Poppy was shown as in need of adoption from Immingham Dogs' Home. As soon as I saw her photo I knew we were a match. I completed the application and was delighted to be invited to meet her. She was absolutely beautiful, sat nicely as we greeted each other and was well beyond my expectations so I went shopping in preparation and the next day I went to collect her. This was our first challenge. She was absolutely terrified in the car but we made it home and she enjoyed exploring her new surroundings. She still struggles with car journeys and I put this down to the very long journey she had in a van from Romania.

Initially Poppy was very nervous but she gradually made herself at home. Of course there were teething problems before she learnt not to chew the furniture and every shoe she could find. If I had to go out without her I left her in the wet room as there wasn't much she could damage or destroy although she had fun with the loo rolls and munched on a few towels. She quickly accepted that she would go in the wetroom with her bed if I was going out. It wasn't many weeks before I could trust her sufficiently to leave her the run of downstairs.

She has always been brilliant on the lead but on the beach she can run free and I know she will come back to me. She loves doing zoomies, playing in the water and lying down in it too. She can swim but prefers being able to touch the bottom with her paws. I have let her off lead in other places but something has caught her interest, such as a hare, and she has raced off over the fields in pursuit. She did eventually come back but it was a very long wait! She is very curious and likes to explore but she seems to have accepted that we do this together now. She likes spotting foxes, cats and squirrels and is learning not to chase them.

Eight months on Poppy and I are almost inseparable. She comes nearly everywhere with me. She loves to be close with me and will lie beside my chair although she has an armchair of her own. I love her cuddles and she loves them too. I am planning to get a sofa we can share soon. If I am gardening she wants to be so close that pruning and cutting back is interrupted as I have to put my tools down! I love her to bits and I guess, in her doggy way, that she loves me too.

She communicates really well and likes her favourite treats best dipped in dog peanut butter. If I give her a treat without the added extra she will drop it, eye point the peanut butter and lick her lips! She can tell the time and as we walk regularly at 08.00, 12.00, 16.00 and 20.00 she will nudge me to tell me it is walk time. She has started to take an interest in balls. She will chase after a ball then run off with it and play with it on her own. Maybe one day it will become a more conventional game of fetch.

Poppy has made such a difference to my life. There is little time for boring chores like housework as we are busy enjoying walks in wild places. I smile frequently nowadays at her funny antics and I believe she is happy too. She is a good reason to get up early and she is wonderful company. She has given me renewed purpose and I really value her companionship. I think we are well matched and we both benefit greatly from being together.

Right now Poppy is telling me it is time for her 20.00 walk. She is absolutely right so I will close now to take her out again.

Rebecca & Fly

At the beginning of August, we decided it was time to welcome another rescue dog into our lives. My sister-in-law Tina had just started fostering one of the dogs from Immingham Dogs Home, a sweet dog named Sherif, and that's when the idea first took root. We already had a Border Collie, but in May, I lost Roxy, my 15-year-old Collie, who had been my world. Her passing left a gaping hole in my heart. Losing her was like losing a piece of myself, and I hadn't quite figured out how to fill that emptiness. So, when Tina brought Sherif home, I couldn't help but get excited at the thought that maybe he could be our new boy.

We arranged to meet Sherif, and I was eager and full of hope that this might be the start of a new chapter for us. The moment I saw him, I felt a connection. He was charming and sweet, and my little girl adored him. Our other dog, Tasha, who is usually a bit of a grump, surprised us by taking a liking to him, too. Normally, she's not interested in making new friends, especially with other dogs, so this was a big deal. But despite all these positives, my husband didn't say much. I've been with him long enough to know when he's into something and when he's not. His silence spoke volumes, and I sensed that maybe Sherif wasn't the one for us after all.

Just as we were leaving the meet-and-greet, my dad called. He mentioned that a friend of his was considering rehoming his Border Collie. The timing seemed almost too perfect. I agreed to go and meet the dog right away to see if he might be the one.

When we arrived, it was love at first sight. He was everything I'd hoped for: beautiful, loyal and loving. I could immediately picture him in our home, filling the void that Roxy had left behind. We told my dad's friend that we'd be happy to take him in, but deep down, I had a feeling he wouldn't be able to let go. Sure enough, the next day, he called to say he'd changed his mind. He couldn't bear to part with his dog, and honestly, I understood. Still, it was a let-down, and I couldn't help but feel disappointed.

At that point, it became clear that Sherif wasn't meant for us, and we turned our attention to finding the perfect Border Collie. I knew it was the right decision, but it was hard to start the search again, especially after getting so close to my dad's friend's dog. I wasn't sure if we'd ever find the right one, and that thought was disheartening.

Then, just a few days later, something incredible happened. I was tagged in a video on the Facebook page. The video featured a dog named Fly, and from the moment I saw him, I felt something special. I showed the video to my husband, and we both knew instantly that this was our dog. It was as if all the pieces had finally fallen into place. There was no doubt, no hesitation, just a quiet certainty that Fly was meant to be part of our family.

We arranged to meet Fly on Saturday, August 3rd, with the plan of bringing him home after our holiday on the 17th if everything went well. But when we met him, we were completely smitten. He was even more wonderful in person than we'd imagined. There was an immediate bond, and we knew we couldn't wait two weeks to bring him home. My other dog, Tasha, usually takes her time warming up to new dogs, seemed to instantly like Fly. That alone was a miracle. Instead of sticking to our original plan, we decided to take Fly home that very day. It felt like it was meant to be.

From the moment we brought Fly home, he fitted right in. A week later, we took him on holiday to Northumberland. It was a good test, really. We wanted to see how he'd handle being away from home and how he'd adapt to new surroundings. On the first day of the holiday, we had a bit of a mishap with a training lead, which left me with rope burns around my ankles and nearly sent my child flying. But Fly's focus on his ball kept him close by when we let him off the lead, and it was clear that he would be a fantastic addition to our family. He stayed by our side, just as Roxy used to, and I couldn't have been happier.

As I sit here now, back in Northumberland, with Fly curled up next to me, I can't help but feel that everything happened for a reason. Losing Roxy was one of the hardest things I've ever been through, but I believe she somehow led us to Fly. It's as if she knew that he was the one who could help heal my heart. Fly has brought so much joy back into our lives, and it's clear that he was the missing piece we needed. My other dog, Tasha, who usually keeps her distance from other dogs, has taken to Fly in a way I never expected. She hasn't growled at him once, which is a miracle in itself. In fact, when they're apart, she'll go up to him and give him little kisses when they're reunited. It's the sweetest thing to watch, making me love him even more.

Fly has genuinely made our lives complete again. There's nothing I could say against him; he's our dream dog. The bond we've formed in such a short time is incredible, and I feel so lucky to have him. Looking back, it's clear that everything worked out exactly as it should. Even though the journey to finding him had its ups and downs, it all led us to the perfect dog. I'm so grateful to Immingham Dogs Home for bringing Fly into our lives. He's helped to heal my heart and brought joy back into our home. It feels like Roxy sent him to us as if she knew that Fly was the one who could fill the void she left behind.

In the end, I know that Fly was meant to be ours. He's more than just a dog; he's a part of our family, and I can't imagine life without him. Thank you, Immingham Dogs Home, for everything you've done. Fly is exactly what we needed; we're so thankful to have him in our lives.

Tina, Simon and Barney [Sherif]

A Tail of Laughter, Love, and a Few Lost Knickers.

It all started with a tag. You know the kind: the one that usually sends you spiralling down a rabbit hole of adorable dog photos, leaving you wondering if you really do need to pay that electric bill this month or if you can squeeze in another fur baby instead.

My sister-in-law, ever the enabler, tagged me in a post from Immingham Dogs Home. Now, she's notorious for tagging me in rescue posts, and believe me, if I could, I'd be running a zoo by now. But this one was different. It wasn't just another post filled with irresistible puppy eyes; it was an urgent call for a foster home to free up kennel space for some older dogs. The timing seemed perfect; I was on summer holidays with plenty of time on my hands. So, I showed the post to Simon, my husband, and without much deliberation, we both agreed. We could do this. We could actually help this time.

The post was about two dogs, Ollie and Sherif. I messaged Kelly, the rescue coordinator, who assured us both boys were friendly and loved other dogs. A crucial detail, given that we already have two big rescue boys: Theo, who is about as social as a cat at a dog show, and Badger, who thinks he's the king of every hill, mole or otherwise. Theo had a rough start in life, surviving on the streets of Romania before making his way to us. The outside world can still be a bit too much for him sometimes, but in his safe spaces, he's the sweetest, most loving boy you could ask for. He needs time to warm up to new things; when he does, he adores other dogs with all his heart. At that moment, we were also dog-sitting my dad's elderly collie, Oscar. So, yeah, our house was about to become a canine convention, and the new recruit had to be a social butterfly or at least not a troublemaker.

By that evening, we'd passed our home check and scheduled an appointment to meet the boys the next day. Now, Theo is not exactly the life of the party, and taking him to the rescue would have been like dragging a cat to a bath. So, we decided it was best to leave him at home and take Badger along. With Badger strapped in, we made the one-hour trek to Immingham Dogs Home. Kelly met us at the gate, took one look at Badger, and suggested Ollie based on size alone. I couldn't argue; Badger is basically a small bear with a wagging tail.

We met Ollie first, and let's say it wasn't love at first sight. Ollie took one sniff of Badger and decided he wasn't a fan. Maybe it was Badger's boisterous energy, or maybe Ollie didn't like the cut of his jib. Either way, it wasn't going to work. So, we tried with Sherif. Out he came, small and unassuming, almost like a pocket-sized superhero. He walked up to Badger with all the confidence of a dog twice his size. Within seconds, they played, sniffed, and marked every available surface. It was a match. I could see that this tiny dynamo would fit right into our chaos.

The only hiccup? Sherif was nervous around men, especially my husband. But that was okay. We figured we could work on that. Kelly kindly provided a harness and collar that fit his petite frame, and off we went, with me in the backseat sandwiched between two dogs. The most adorable thing happened on that ride home: Sherif and Badger curled up together and slept, cuddled like long-lost brothers. My heart melted.

When we got home, we introduced Sherif to Theo and Oscar individually. To our delight, it went off without a hitch. Sherif's tail wagged so hard I thought it might fly off. As the excitement died down, Sherif found a cosy spot under the stairs and declared it his safe haven. We set up a little bedroom for him there, complete with a new bed that Simon picked up from Costco, and for the next few days, Sherif barely left his den. We put up a pet gate so he could have his own space to decompress, and he seemed content to observe the household from his little nook.

Over the next few days, Sherif started to cling to me like Velcro. He was clearly more comfortable around women, and my husband was determined to win him over. Simon would sit on the floor, speaking softly to him, offering treats, and taking him for walks. It was slow going, but we could see progress. Meanwhile, I was getting attached. Fast.

On the third day, I found myself posting pictures of Sherif on Facebook, trying to find him a forever home. But that night, as I sat under the stairs with Sherif, tears streaming down my face, Simon found me. I was a mess, hiccupping sobs, red-faced, and clutching this tiny dog like he was the last bit of happiness in the world. Simon knelt beside me, and instead of teasing, he wrapped his arms around us both. "I knew from the start he wasn't going anywhere," he whispered, his voice thick with emotion. "You were never going to let him go." It turns out Simon had more faith in my soft heart than I did. We decided then and there that Sherif wasn't leaving. He was ours. And just like that, our family grew by four paws.

The next day, I messaged Kelly to break the news: Sherif had found his forever home, right here with us. We were ecstatic. My niece was over the moon, and we couldn't wait to tell everyone. But Sherif wasn't responding to his name, so we decided to rename him Barney. It didn't take long for him to catch on. Barney was officially part of the family.

Now, if you think adopting a rescue dog is all heartwarming moments and wagging tails, let me tell you about the ninth circle of doggy hell: housebreaking.

Barney is as adorable as they come, but his idea of a toilet is... let's say, creative. We're talking about the kitchen floor, living room rug, and even that one fancy cushion I thought would be safe on the top of the sofa. You'd think by now I'd have learned that nothing is out of reach for a determined dog with short legs and a long reach. Simon and I have become experts at the "uh-oh sniff", a technique where you scan the room with your nose for the faint whiff of trouble.

But Barney's antics don't stop at creative toileting. No, his true talent lies in his ability to reduce me to tears of laughter and sometimes frustration. Let's talk about the 'great knicker caper'. I've lost more pairs of knickers to Barney's games than I care to admit. There's something about my underwear drawer that calls to him like a siren song. He will fish them out, prance around the house like he's won the lottery, and then, when he's sufficiently proud of his haul, rope Badger into a tug-of-war match. Seeing those two hooligans playing tug-of-war with my knickers makes me laugh until I cry, though I'm not sure the neighbours find it quite as amusing when I'm out hanging laundry.

Then there was the time with my brand-new cardigan. It was fresh out of the packaging, hung up neatly over the living room door to air out. I thought it was safe. I was wrong. We came home to find Barney strutting around the house with my cardigan in his mouth, dragging it like a trophy while Badger did his best to wrestle it away. By the time we retrieved it, my cardigan looked like Swiss cheese. I suppose it's my own fault for thinking anything in this house is safe. Lesson learned, right? Wrong. Because a week later, he got into my sock drawer. I swear, Barney has a future in fashion, specifically in the distressed, pre-chewed look.

But even with all the chaos, we wouldn't have it any other way. Barney is settling in beautifully. That timid little dog who first came into our lives is blossoming into a confident, cheeky character who's winning us all over, one day at a time. Simon is making great strides with him, too. Barney now runs to him at the first sound of a treat bag crinkling.

We're planning our first trip to the beach soon, and I can't wait to see Barney's reaction to the sand and surf. He's already proven to be a joy to take out and about, earning compliments left and right. We're also looking forward to introducing him to doggy daycare, where he can socialise to his heart's content.

Though this wasn't an intentional adoption, we can't imagine life without Barney now. He's become an integral part of Team Hayhurst, and it feels like he was always meant to be here. My grandma always used to say, 'Everything happens for a reason', and I believe that with all my heart. Barney's journey to us was a bit of a happy accident, but it's clear he was meant to find his way into our home and hearts.

So, here's to Barney's future with us. Thank you, Immingham Dogs Home, for bringing him into our lives. He's already filled our home with so much joy, laughter, and a few chewed-up knickers. But most importantly, he's found his forever home. We're so grateful, and we can't wait to see what adventures lie ahead for Barney and the rest of The Hayhurst crew.

Kim & Pippy [Pippa]

We had seen Pippa bouncing about and being her bubbly self on Facebook posts. She had always caught our eye and was currently in a temporary foster placement. We had decided that we weren't ready for another dog but admired and supported Immingham Dogs Home in any way we could.

After I completed the Grimsby 10k to raise some funds for the home, I popped in to drop some collection pots off and asked if I could meet her. That was it; she was in my heart!

My husband was so jealous I got a chance to meet the dogs, so we took another drive down and walked Pippy. When I saw him walking her and how happy they seemed, I just knew she was for us.

Obviously, with three kids, we had to make sure that they were compatible, so we took the kids to meet Pip. She charmed the pants off them, too! When my daughter said, 'I think she's my dog', the deal was done. We picked her up to offer her a foster placement.

Over the next few weeks, we were waiting, expecting something to happen or go wrong. We'd had a rough year and faced some awful disappointments. We needed something positive to happen.

During difficult times, she sits by my feet, silent but there as if she knows I need company. When my son came home upset, she went straight to him, trying to cuddle him. She adores the kids, and they find a sense of comfort in knowing that she is there. We were scared it would not work out and would be another heartbreak for us as a family.

We waited and waited, but this girl was just a dream! She was so lovely and a bit goofy! She fitted right in with the family. After a few weeks, we couldn't remember her not being with us.

When the time came for us to go on holiday, the kennels had agreed that she could go back while we were away, but we were heartbroken and worried that she would be sad. The kids were worried that she was going to be 'given away' or adopted and that we would never see her again. We need not have worried, as Pippy took it in her stride and just got on with it.

I was worried she wasn't bothered about us and wouldn't want to return to us. When we arrived back, the kids asked every five minutes, 'When are you getting her?' and 'Is she coming home?'

The house was very quiet without Pippy; it felt like something was missing.

We went to collect her, and she just sidled out as if going for a walk. When she noticed us standing there, she flew to us, crying and jumping excitedly! It was true; she had missed us as much as we missed her.

We returned home to three thrilled children, and she returned to her favourite comfy bed.

It was my 40th birthday the next day, and my parents arrived with my card. It contained her adoption fee; they knew how much we missed her. My mother is currently terminally ill, and

Pippy may be the last gift that she ever gives me. I find comfort in knowing that she will leave a piece of love with us in Pippy when she's gone.

When we get up or come home from shopping or work, she is always there, ready for a cuddle. She is like sunshine for the soul.

It turns out we needed her more than she needed us.

Lorna and Buttons

After losing Biscuit, my Springer Spaniel, his little brother Scamp, the Cavalier King Charles seemed to be okay, and I thought one dog would be enough.

I'd been staying with friends and their dogs for the last two years and finally moved into my own place. As all doggy parents do, I bought a camera to keep an eye on him when I went out, and what I saw broke my heart.

Seeing him cry and bark constantly without a playmate for company was awful, and I knew I needed to get him a new friend.

I've been following Immingham Dogs Home for months. I love seeing all the dogs and being able to do my bit by sharing on social media when I can or even donating to the dogs there who need help.

I started actively looking, and I made a list of dogs that would be suitable for Scamp and me.

I needed a small-medium dog that would be happy with a few walks a day around me working from home but also be okay chilling and relaxing while I did my work. I wanted something small, so it meant I could rent easily with them both, and others wouldn't mind looking after him when I was away.

I got in touch about two dogs, and one had already been adopted. I was slightly disappointed, but I took a chance when they said Buttons was in a foster home and that I could arrange to meet him.

I was nervous and said to myself, 'I don't have to say yes; we're just seeing if he gets along with Scamp'. I was going in open-mindedly, as I didn't know if I was ready for another dog. But the minute I met Buttons, I knew he was going to be mine.

He was a dream to walk, and he got along fine with Scamp. It was perfect. I was so excited. He ticked all my boxes as I walked around with him and his foster mum, asking all the questions about him.

"How does he do in the car and on journeys?"

"How is he with other dogs?"

"What is he like during the day?" Etc.

When we returned to the house, I left Scamp in the car; I wanted to see how Buttons was with all the dogs at the foster home.

He was nervous and barking, but the minute I sat on the floor and spoke to him and brought out treats, he showed his cheeky little side and did zoomies, and my heart melted. I knew I had to have him. He had the sweetest soul.

The next weekend, I picked him up. He was nervous and scared, and so was I.

I'd never owned a rescue dog before, and I'd done all the googling on how to get him settled, leave him with his own time, how long it would take for him to get settled, what could happen, and what I should do. I tried everything I could to get ready to be the best forever home for him.

The first week or two was challenging and upsetting, as he

cowered and spent all his time in his cage. I made sure to remember that he was settling, and it wasn't me.

I didn't know much about his background besides that he was from Romania. I had no clue what type of dog he was; I had to get an app to tell me 'Jack Russell and Australian Kelpie' just to put on his insurance forms. I couldn't get my head around how anyone could mistreat a dog so severely that he'd cower at being touched, be fearful when told to sit, run away when being given a treat, and see the sadness and discomfort in his eyes and body.

When out on walks, he became 'reactive' to other dogs, and I was so scared I would have another reactive dog again [my springer was bitten when he was four and was reactive for the rest of his life].

I knew I had to get some help as soon as possible, so I contacted a local dog trainer, Quality Canines, to help assess him. He was nervous and quiet and wouldn't listen. He wouldn't eat treats or do anything. The assessment outcome was that he was nervous and scared, and that's why he was barking and lunging, not that he was aggressive or reactive. I sighed the biggest relief. I can work with shy and nervous dogs.

As the weeks went by, he came more and more out of his shell. He would give cuddles, do little zoomies, and get excited when I came home or when I'd come downstairs in the morning, as he was happier sleeping downstairs.

His little personality grew; he was such a gentle soul. He would be gently jumping up at you, pawing at you to remind you that he wanted all the attention, his signature butt in the air and head down to show his excitement, along with his little wiggles and spins.

Seeing him grow and learn has been the most fulfilling and beautiful thing.

I thought I'd find it much harder than it has been, but he's fitted in like a dream.

Learning his mannerisms and behaviour in and out of the house. How he is with dogs and people, and how he manages guests in the house or knocks at the front door. He sleeps and plays and chases cats and birds. He has his chosen dog friends, and he loves his walks.

It's only been four months with us since January 2024, but it feels like so much longer. I wouldn't be without him and his little brother [not really little brother because he's eleven and Buttons is four]. He's growing, changing, and learning every single day, and I'm just so happy he is comfortable, building his confidence and showing his love and affection.

What's really been a game changer with him recently are one-on-one little adventures, walks, and road trips. On these one-on-one trips with him, he returned happier and more attentive, would listen to commands, and learned more, like going to bed and cuddling up with me, going up to more dogs, and not barking as much. Honestly, it's been amazing for him, and I'd encourage anyone to adopt a rescue if you can.

Buttons now goes to social classes where he can off-lead play and make friends, and has come out of his shell eight months on. He plays with toys, loves his food and walks, and loves going to the field. He's settled in, bonded deeply with me, and he's even better than I could ever have imagined. Seeing his personality grow, along with his confidence, makes me swell with pride and happiness every single day. I'm honoured to have him as my dog. He'll never be treated badly again.

I'm excited to see how he and our bond will grow in another four to six months.

Thank you for letting me share our story with you.

Rach, Shirl & Basil [Ted]

My partner and I lost one of our dogs at the beginning of the lockdown to kidney failure. Over a few weeks, we realised that our eight-year-old Westie looked lost, and our house felt very odd with only one dog.

We started looking at charities that rescued dogs from abroad and eventually came across Amicii Dog Rescue. After contacting them, we were sent a couple of possible matches, and Basil immediately caught our eye.

He was staying at Immingham Dogs Home near Grimsby, so we arranged a time to go and see him; he was about eighteen months old and had just had an eye removed. He looked perfect on the video that was sent; he was very playful and was running after a ball and bringing it back to Kelly [she obviously taught him this trick to create a good impression, as he's never brought a ball back since then!].

The first visit didn't go well; he was so excited to see our dog that he ran up to us, and Layla, the resident dog, immediately pinned him to the floor! We took him out for a walk with Layla, who wasn't happy and continuously told him that she was happy being an only dog, but if he insisted on tagging along, she was going to be the 'top dog'. On this first meeting, he also became spooked by a digger and dragged, pulled and hopped like a kangaroo to get back to the kennels; it took all my partner's strength to hold on to his lead. He was pulling that badly. But despite this, something was pulling on the heart-strings that made us want to keep trying.

We persevered and made two more 160-mile round trips that week to visit and take him for a walk. By the third trip, Layla looked to be 'tolerating' him, so we asked Kelly if we could take him home on trial for a couple of weeks.

When we got home, he quickly found his favourite spot, on the sofa! At first, we put him in the crate at night for his own safety but realised after a time that he and Layla were becoming inseparable as long as she could be 'top dog'. We quickly fell head over heels in love with him despite his nervousness and ear-shattering bark, and deep down, we knew he would be staying permanently.

We also realised that our house had now become his 'safe-haven' and nobody, but nobody, was allowed through the gate, not even the grandchildren: every cloud and all that. My partner was returning to work soon after the six-week break, and we needed to get Basil to meet Jo, the dog walker, and boy, was that a nightmare! He was introduced outside, went for a walk, etc, and built up a bit of a relationship, but still, he barked for a solid 45 minutes when we brought her into the house for the first time. After a week of us hiding outside when she came, Basil was finally happy, allowing her into the house to take him for a walk. Getting the dog walker into the house safely was the biggest obstacle overcome, so we contacted Kelly to say her had found his forever home.

Layla and Basil have had a few scraps over the four years, some instigated by him [jealousy over humans or food] but mostly by her. After the first scrap [instigated by her], he was inconsolable, but I think over time, he realised that it wasn't the end of the world, and he got over it! They've also had naughty moments together; one time, coming down from a Zoom meeting in the spare room, they'd obviously had a mad half hour as all my diary and notebooks for work were shredded around the front room!

He has relaxed over the years and become a big lump that seems incapable of sitting on the floor when there is a comfy human available to lie on. He is now a very chilled and affectionate dog with people he knows and has been known to fall asleep on new people.

'Unfortunately', he has also accepted the grandkids as part of the pack, and they are not only allowed in the house but are allowed to move off the sofa. All good things come to an end! It is still an issue when somebody new comes into the house; whilst not ferocious now, he has gotten into the habit of barking. Most people who know him accept that he will woof for a bit while wagging his tail [which is very extensive!] and eventually shut up.

Going out was a bit stressful at times; in the evening, he was desperate to get home again, and we still struggled to get him out after a certain time.

Adopting Basil has been one of the best things we've done; it's a joy to see him trust a new person or be less stressed about certain things that used to terrify him. He's a bit chubbier than he was when we first got him, but everyone who knows him is amazed at how different he is now.

This story cannot really explain how much pleasure and love Basil has brought to our lives and how grateful we are that charities such as Amicii and Immingham Dogs Home give these dogs a better life.

Rebecca, Malcolm, Angela and Tawny [Toby]

We lost our beautiful Border Collie, Jasper, having had him for fourteen years from when he was a puppy. He was our loyal and faithful friend and constant shadow. It was a devastating and sudden loss, and one we all struggled with. We still miss him every day, as he was a part of our family.

The house felt so empty without him, his greetings when we arrived home, and his verbal joy when playing with his favourite toys. We tried to continue walking without him, but it was so hard to meet people who would ask where Jasper was, and our lead hands felt so empty.

We thought long and hard about whether to get another dog: we felt the house was too empty and quiet, and walks were no longer enjoyable. We scoured all the usual sites and were amazed and saddened to see how many dogs needed homes. Although we had Jasper from a puppy and at that time really wanted a Border Collie [having grown up with them], we felt that with so many dogs in rescue centres, we should look there as we felt we could provide a loving home.

It was by chance that we found Immingham Dogs Home after considering other rescues and looking at lots of photos of dogs needing homes. Little Tawny [previous Toby] popped up on this occasion, and we immediately thought he was so cute and handsome. He was a much smaller dog than we were used to, but he seemed to have a big personality.

We filled in the questionnaire with our desire to adopt but didn't really hold out much hope. He looked such a cutie, and we were sure there would be a lot of interest in him. It was a very pleasant surprise when we received the call from the Dogs Home asking us to provide a video showing our home and garden, etc., to see if we were suitable.

The visit to meet Tawny went very well; he certainly raced around the paddock and lived up to his 'pocket rocket' description. Having been given treats for him, he came over to say hello, and we just thought he was the cutest little chap, with the most beautiful large, expressive brown eyes [which Malcolm refers to as his Puss in Boots eyes]. We decided there and then that we would very much like to adopt him, and thankfully, Kelly agreed we were suitable. He happily trotted off with Kelly, and we agreed to collect him in a week.

With much excitement, we duly purchased the essentials needed to bring him home, including a new bed, name tag, collar, and, of course, food and toys [we went a little overboard on the toys and treats!]. We also purchased a dog seat for the car to clip him in safely.

The day to pick Tawny up arrived, and we eagerly arrived at the rescue to collect him. Kelly brought Tawny out to the car, where we realised the harness was slightly too small [although he is only a little chap, he is very long]. That problem was soon resolved, and he happily sat in his little seat. We sat with him as Kelly was unsure how he'd cope with the journey. As it turned out, he was a little superstar, looking curiously at us and outside the car window.

Once home he took to exploring up and downstairs, as well as the garden. We had been warned that we probably wouldn't have anything, such as birds, etc, in the garden for long with Tawny around, and that was certainly the case. He immediately took to seeing off the wood pigeons, and he has a very commanding bark for such a small pooch! We also discovered how high he could jump and understood the need to say how high our fences were. Having had a dog who was obsessed with tennis balls, we decided to see if Tawny would be interested in playing with them, and wow, was he interested! Not only was he extremely fast, we felt sure we had adopted a part kangaroo! Those little back legs are very deceptive.

On the first night, he immediately went into his bed, which, for some reason, seemed amazingly cute and gratifying to us. He was a little unsettled the first couple of nights, but once he had checked his territory and marked the garden accordingly, he became more relaxed. His favourite place to rest now [if it's not occupied] is Malcolm's chair!

The first walks were very interesting as he would bark and lunge at any traffic, but that has dramatically improved [although he will still take on the odd tractor]. We had been used to a strong, sometimes stubborn Border Collie and felt sure that Tawny was part Collie, part Terrier and, as mentioned before, part kangaroo! However, we have now been told he is probably of the Kokoni breed. He is extremely intelligent and also very loving to us all.

He is the gentlest boy with his food, which he thoroughly enjoys. However, when given a treat that maybe isn't quite wanted at that time, he will proceed to store it in his larder for later [i.e., a suitable plant pot, whether full of plants or not, for a later feast]. If he notices us watching him, he will give up on his task and give us a look as if to say, 'I'm not up to anything, honest!'

He loves attention, gives lots of love back, and adores belly rubs. Almost immediately after we brought him home, he rolled over onto his back with his little legs splayed out. This appears to be his favourite default position! He also performs his wiggly worm dance across the floor, and his happy 'zoomies' are a sight to behold.

Tawny is a very vocal dog and will alert us to all possible intruders, whether they happen to be just shutting their car door or walking past the house. Consequently, we have lovely dog nose art on the windows. However, he just ensures we are all safe and where we should be.

Initially, he would bark at other dogs on walks, but now he is so happy to see his regular friends. Even new acquaintances may get a bark followed by a cry of 'Can I say hello?' He gets so excited when he sees his lady friends [one of whom is also a Romanian rescue] that he cannot contain himself with his little legs going a hundred miles an hour.

We have had Tawny for about ten months now and cannot imagine life without him. He has proved to be such a little character, full of life, and has settled very well into our home and family. He makes us laugh every day with his antics and cheeky personality. He has gone through quite a number of toys and is always pleased with himself when they no longer resemble toys and their stuffing surrounds him! He also doubles as a flycatcher in his spare time.

We decided to change his name to Tawny, given that his beautiful colouring and markings reminded us of a Tawny owl, and thankfully, he very quickly responded to his new name. His other names include 'Tawny Tornado' [the zoomies] and 'Tawny Boots' [his little white leg socks].

We would just like to say a big thank you to Kelly and all

her staff for the wonderful work they do for these dogs and for allowing us to adopt such an amazing little dog who brings us such joy every day!

Mick, Sally, Sidney and Astro

Mick saw a photo of Astro in late February 2022 and instantly fell in love with him. His beautiful, thick black-and-white coat and gorgeous but sad face made Mick want to go collect him and bring him home immediately. Mick was drawn to something about Astro's photos.

After losing our other two five years earlier, I wasn't ready to have another dog, and I said that if Mick wanted him, Astro would be his dog. I was really against it, but just because I wasn't ready didn't mean our home wasn't ready for a dog.

Shortly after, Kelly brought a very scared shell of a dog into our home. Never have we seen a dog so shut down and fearful of human beings. Kelly knew we would be able to care for him and help him, as we had taken in a very scared dog from India before.

Astro spent all his time on his bed and wouldn't look at us or come near us; we had to put his harness on him and carry him into the garden as we couldn't walk him for the first couple of months. We spent many an hour sitting in the garden as he was so scared to be out there by himself.

We had to get help from a dog behaviourist [Quality Canines], and under Natalie's guidance, we slowly gained Astro's trust. To begin with, we couldn't touch or look at him; we fed him and left him to get used to his new environment. The one thing he did very quickly was melt my heart and make sure I knew I was his mummy and Mick was his daddy. He couldn't have received more love from us, and it showed.

When Astro came over from Romania about five months earlier, his brother Sidney was left behind as he couldn't travel due to taking medication for heartworms. Unfortunately, dog imports had been stopped when Sidney was healthy enough to travel. So it was nearly a year after Astro arrived in the UK that Sidney did. We have never seen two dogs from the same litter so different. Astro is a typical black and white collie, whereas Sidney is fudge brown, and we say he looks like a cross between a fox and a hyena.

From day one of having Astro, Mick and Kelly both wanted Sidney to come live with us and Astro, but yet again, I was against it. That was until I saw a photo of Sidney and knew he belonged with his brother and us. He was a mass of fudge brown fur with the most beautiful eyes, so when Sidney arrived in the UK at Christmas 2022, he had Christmas presents waiting under our tree from Santa Paws.

On the days that Sidney was on the transport driving over from Romania, we constantly updated the message thread to see where they were.

The day the boys were reunited was amazing; they howled and jumped all over each other and chased each other around the house, and then, bizarrely, they ignored each other for three days. It was hard work to start with, but so worth it.

We utilised all the knowledge we had learned to train Astro with Sidney so we didn't overwhelm him. The biggest thing we noticed was how much Astro protected Sidney [and still does].

When Sidney is feeling scared or unsure of something, Astro senses it and always jumps in front of him to give him reassurance and protection. It's a beautiful thing to see, so because of this, we always called Astro the big brother.

Sidney didn't like going on walkies to start with and pulled his hardest to get back home, but he slowly got a little more confident and now loves going on walkies over the old golf course with his brother.

We have taken them on many little holidays to the seaside, and they love travelling in the car to see family in the Midlands. Their favourite thing to do is go for walks down at the boating lake at the end of Cleethorpes and call into the Brew Stop for their breakfast of doggie sausage.

Both boys are still scared of most people, but once they trust you, they love you with all their hearts. They love to play chase with each other and do zoomies around the freedom field with their fur friends.

They have been back to stay in the kennels a few times, and each time they do, their confidence grows.

The boys have boxes full of teddies and toys and can freely roam our home. They can decide where and with whom they sleep. We couldn't ask for more loving dogs. They bring us such love and laughs, as they have their own unique characters. Being adopted by Astro and Sidney is the best thing that could have happened. As time passes, their characters develop even more, and now they show it to other people, which, to start with, they didn't.

They say that dogs choose you and not the other way around, and it's definitely true in our case. Astro and Sidney are so much like our other two dogs we used to have that we always say that our fur baby girls [Scraps and Rani] chose the boys for us as they knew our home and hearts needed them in it.

We call the boys Prince Astro and Prince Sidney. Our first

dog, Scraps, was our little princess, so we named our Indian dog Rani, which means queen in Hindi. Thus, we have our own doggie royal family. We have caricature drawings of them wearing crowns.

An added bonus of getting Astro and Sidney was that we both got involved as volunteers at the dogs' home. It's a joy to help other dogs find their fur-ever homes and raise much-needed funds.

Rose, Kevin & Millie

A couple of years after losing our last dog we still felt unsure if we were ready for another one. We heard that Immingham Dogs Home needed foster homes for some of their dogs. As we have previously fostered children, we decided we would apply. We had our home check and made an appointment to see Kelly with regards to fostering a dog.

We arrived at the allotted time and mentioned to Kelly that we had seen one dog online that we were interested in. Kelly, unfortunately, said that the dog had been reserved for adoption. We continued chatting and discussed another dog we had also seen online. All the time we were chatting, Kelly had a little dog in her arms. It looked very frightened; Kelly said it was a rescue from Romania. We agreed that we would take the dog home to foster. Kelly gave us some food to start us off, saying they were trying to get her to eat dry food, but she wasn't too keen. We took a little of each with us.

We previously had only had male, medium to large dogs, this was a small female dog called Millie. We put Millie in the car, and I sat with her on my lap until we got home; she shook all the way.

On arrival, Millie was happy to come indoors with us; it was no problem. She mooched around the rooms in our bungalow and then went into the enclosed garden. We didn't have a dog bed, so we improvised with a single quilt, which she immediately took to, and it is still her favourite. Kevin later made her wooden raised beds, one in the lounge and one for the bedroom. Millie also has an outdoor, raised, covered sunbed with a cooling mat. She is a proper spoilt doggy, lol.

Millie would come to us, but on her terms. She initially spent most of her indoor time on her quilt bed.

She continued shaking, and it was a couple of weeks before she seemed at ease with us. She always ate her meals, and we eventually got her onto dry food. Millie, at first, didn't like visitors and would even nip their ankles as they came in. There seemed no reason as to who or why. Men and women were targets. Later, a visit to the vet gave us clues as to why. She had also started coming to sit with us on the settee and loved being stroked.

We had a couple of 'accidents' in the house for the first two days, but nothing since. I believe that Millie has at some time been living indoors somewhere. After two weeks, we made another appointment to see Kelly, this time to say that we wanted to adopt Millie. We had started to fall in love with her.

Millie's passport put her date of birth as 2/2/20, making her four years of age. She was neutered and chipped, which was transferred to us on adoption.

We noticed that Millie continued shaking and took her to the vet for a check-up. She was diagnosed with an ear infection and was given drops and an ear wash. It seemed to improve, but after a few weeks, it was getting worse again. She needed to be sedated so that they could inspect her ears properly and clean them. We were told that both of her eardrums were perforated and bleeding internally, and she was put on steroids. Millie is still on them months later but on a lower dose and doesn't currently have any problems, and the ankle nipping has stopped, too. On her first visit, the vet muzzled Millie, but she let him do whatever he needed without any fuss; he has never muzzled her since and said she is such a lovely dog.

Millie loves her walks, especially at the beach where I let her off the lead, but she walks lovely on the lead, too, luckily. We do not live far away from the beach. She is food-driven because of the steroids and will forage for edibles on our walks. Her recall can be hit and miss if she thinks there is food around, but I pop her back on her lead for a short while, and it seems to improve again. Millie tolerates other dogs in and out of the house; we have dogs that visit and sometimes stay over, and she doesn't bother. Unfortunately, after lots of encouragement, she still doesn't play with any type of toys or other dogs.

She is actually frightened by many of the toys, bless her, especially the squeaky ones. She is a great guard dog and barks at all arrivals to our door, stopping very quickly if she recognises them, even better if they have a treat for her. We often call into a neighbour after our walk, and she even knows where the neighbour keeps her treats and sits in the cupboard waiting for her to give them to her.

Everyone that meets her thinks she is a lovely dog, and if they start to chat to us, Millie just sits and waits patiently until we move on again. She has even been known to sit next to people if out on a walk and they are sitting eating, say, outside a cafe or on the beach. She looks longingly at them, hoping they will give her something. I make a point of keeping her away if there is a picnic as I'm sure she would join in uninvited, which could be disastrous.

Millie has turned into a very lovable, cheeky little dog, but we love her, and she fits into our family perfectly. If she sees you trying to go on your phone or computer when we are sat on the settee, she jumps up for attention and walks on the keyboard. She travels really well in the car and has never tried to destroy anything within the home or anywhere else we have taken her. She sits lovely in a cafe or at the pub when we visit them. We have been on many cottage or hotel breaks, and she always behaves. Although she was very wary of stairs to start with, she doesn't have a problem with them now. She follows us at home and likes to be with us but is equally happy being left if we go out without her. We have had her since March 2023 and have no regrets whatsoever.

Just Joey [extract]

There were people everywhere.

All above me: ignoring me.

They were around Dad's bed.

He was being taken, not roughly, and he wasn't protesting. But he couldn't.

I needed to stop them.

But I was too small.

I was picked up; I kicked, and I bit.

I quietened as the other people left.

I looked at the bed. There was a dent where he had been. A warm spot I would sometimes curl into, smell his scent, relax and fall back to sleep until I was called for breakfast. I tried to scramble free to get to that spot, to feel warm and safe. But I was held close and taken from the room.

I cried.

* * *

I shivered and curled up tighter: it was minus two degrees, and I was not in my comfy bed. I wasn't even in my house.

Or with my family.

I was in a cell.

Concrete walls and floors stank of disinfectant, and there was a warm breeze from somewhere.

It was dark. I heard others breathing, but no one was there with me. I curled up on my bedding; at least, this was mine. It smelled of Dad and helped me relax.

I heard activity. Footsteps came along the passageway, and I blinked as the winter sun came through the bars on the windows. The latch was lifted on my cell. I edged back into the corner, frightened of what was to come. Two bowls were placed before me. My nose twitched: biscuits and water. The rosy-cheeked girl who had brought them in ruffled my fur, smiled and left; onto the next. I edged my way towards the bowls sniffing the air before them. It smelled good, and I took a small mouthful. I was not really hungry as I felt sad more than anything. But I ate a little before curling back into the corner of my bed, tucked my nose under my leg, and cried quietly.

The daily routine was the same. The nice girls came in and fed me; they always smiled, cuddled me, and spoke to me in comforting tones. I didn't understand what they were saying, but they were kind.

They were friendly, but I didn't like being there and missed my dad. Where was he? The rosy-cheeked girl clipped a lead on me, walked me down the corridor past other cells, and led me into the grassy paddock. My nose twitched, and my tail gave a slight wag. I could smell other dogs, horses, and, I twitched again, cats! I wandered around, sniffing here and there and marking the territory. There was an old boy in the corner, an Alsatian. His fur was dull and in clumps; he was very old indeed. He limped from stiff-

ness in his back legs when he got up to walk. He was almost blind, so he sensed his way around the paddock but had been there so long that he rarely bumped into anything. He moved from corner to corner, changing the blurred view from sheep to cars in the car park. This was his home, and he would spend his last days there. We sniffed each other with respect, and I left him alone.

'Rosy Cheeks' called my name, and I glanced at her. She had a lead in her hand, but I continued to sniff around. She called me again, leant forward and patted her knees. I only responded to dad, so I ignored her. She walked over, gently lowered the loop over my head, slid up the toggle, ruffled my head, and gave me a gentle tug on the lead. Walkies. We were out in the countryside; I was not used to all the smells. I came from a town, a busy place with cars and people. Here smelled different; I especially liked the horse pooh and how it clung to my long coat; for some reason, I found that quite comforting. We trudged around the muddy field; my little paws picked their way in the ruts whilst Rosy Cheeks squelched in the mud, sometimes giggling as she got stuck and had to tug her welly out. She talked to me all the time and even sang. I pretended not to take any notice; I just sniffed, scratched at the earth and peed.

When we returned to the cells, she sprayed water on my legs, dried me, and brushed my coat. I wouldn't say I liked being brushed, but I let her do it. The less fuss I made, the sooner I went home.

* * *

"Blooming phone when I'm trying to draw." I looked at the caller, Jayne, my neighbour. "Hi, Hun. Are you still interested in a dog?"

"Er, yes, of course. Why?"

"Think we've found you one. Come to the pub, and we'll take you to see him."

The phone went dead. I did that daft thing, looked at it, and then down at myself: PJ bottoms and a sweatshirt. Well, it was Sunday, but now I had better get dressed. The drawing of a Jack Russell would wait until later.

On the 10-minute drive, I wondered what sort of dog they had found, and as I wormed my way through the pub Jayne's three Border Terriers caught sight of me and yapped excitedly. A glass of wine was thrust into my hand, and a stool was vacated for me to sit down. Three wet noses wanted my attention before anything else. I scratched their heads and asked Jayne about the dog.

"Oh, it's so sweet. It's a Cocker Spaniel crossed with a Sheltie, ever so friendly, and it's up at the kennels."

"Long-haired?"

Jayne put her hand on my arm, "I know you didn't want long-haired, but wait until you see him; he's gorgeous." I raised an eyebrow; she knew I was a tough nut to crack and a softie where dogs were concerned. "He's ten years old, and his owner died suddenly. The son had no time for a dog, so he dropped him into the kennels hoping to find a home rather than take him to a sanctuary."

I sipped on my drink and wondered what the heck I was doing. I knew having a dog again would change my life completely. I would be responsible for a living, demanding thing and I still wasn't sure I was ready for that again. But I'd been single for eight years, and there was a gaping hole in my life. My home was devoid of life and love. No man had yet come into my life for more than a blink of an eye, and I was sadly very lonely. With a dog around, I would have a purpose to my days, but was I too set in my ways? There was only one way to find out.

We left the pub for the kennels, and more Border Terriers ran in and out of my legs. A white cat scowled as it walked past and headed for the warmth of my car bonnet. In a paddock of muddy grass, I saw an ancient Alsatian with the glazed eyes of the blind; his nose twitched as he scented the air. I put my hand on the fence, and he nuzzled it. A girl came from the kennels with what looked like a miniature border collie and headed towards us. "This is Joey."

I knelt to say hello; he seemed disinterested. His coat was very long, almost touching the floor. He sniffed at me, and I reached out to fuss him. He looked a little tubby, but my hand sank into a very thick coat of fur: he was a tiny chap underneath it all, standing about 12" high to his shoulder. She gave me the lead, and we headed for a little walk around the field. We plodded in mutual silence; Joey never looked up once. I cut off the top of the field and headed across the tractor tracks to the opposite side; Joey still carefully placed his feet in the tracks but not bothering if there was a puddle in the way; he just plodded straight through it. He seemed such a sad little chap; could I not give him a home?

A week later, I returned. Joey was in the paddock sitting in the opposite corner to the Alsatian; I got out of the car, and he jumped up the fence. Was he pleased to see me? I'm sure I saw a slight wag of the tail.

I had a new collar and lead.

This little boy was coming home with me.

* * *

I heard a car; who was coming today? Was it Dad? I looked across from the paddock, it was That Lady again, and she was laughing with the big man who locked us up at night. She had something in her hand; I put my paws up the fence for a closer look; it was a new collar and lead. Rosy Cheeks came into the paddock and called me. New Lady had given her the collar and lead: they were for me! It had been a long time since I had a new collar, and this one was bright red. Rosy Cheeks led me towards the New Lady and said goodbye with a big hug, then New Lady picked me up and fussed me. She was warm, soft, and scratched behind my ears; I liked that. Then she put me on the seat in her car. She shook hands with the big man and got in the car, and we started moving. I barked.

I barked at the trees as we passed.

I barked at the horses.

I barked, and I barked.

Where were we going?

I was scared and tried to get onto her lap, but she pushed me back, muttering something about 'driving'. We stopped, but I carried on barking. She opened the door and encouraged me out. Grass, bushes, pee. In through a door. Carpet under my feet. I hadn't felt carpet for weeks, so I sniffed it. She took my lead off and talked to me as I sniffed the couch, then the table. I didn't know what she was saying, but she was smiling. I was rooted to the spot, listening: was Dad here? She put a water bowl down, and I drank as she opened another door. The smell of fresh air flooded in, and it was the fresh air I was used to of coal smoke, cars and people. Then I smelled something else and edged towards the door. My nose rose in the air, and my heart beat faster...cats! But I didn't want to go into a cold cell again, and this could be a trap. Should I go out? She walked ahead of me, and I slowly followed. I sniffed around not far from the door, peed and then ran back inside. She laughed. I waited until the door was shut before I drank again. I didn't know where I was or what was happening, but I felt ok here. Maybe Dad would turn up later.

I jumped onto the chair, felt the fluffy cushion under my feet, and curled up to wait.

* * *

I sat and watched him as he slept. He had hardly moved since we came home. I assumed he was unsettled, so I didn't worry about it, but I found it hard to watch TV and relax. He was curled in such a tight ball on the chair that you couldn't see where he started or ended, just a bundle of long fur, asleep but tense; the poor thing. He had been through a lot the last few weeks and must be confused.

I carried on my everyday chores around the house like he wasn't there; he watched every move but stayed curled up tight. I sat down with my dinner on a tray; he raised his head, stretched, sniffed the air, and then curled back up again. A dog not interested in human food? There was a first.

He watched as I put on my shoes and picked up his lead; he started to move, then stopped. I had no idea what he was thinking, but I knew he needed to stretch his legs. I clipped the lead on and led him around the block, allowing him to sniff and pee. Back home, I put his dinner down; he ate some, then curled up in the same chair spot, his eyes peering at me. Before long, he was sound asleep; I hope he felt safe. He started to snore, stretched his legs and twitched; was he chasing something? Then quiet for a short while, his paws twitched again, and he cried. Cries as I'd never heard from a dog, like a kitten mewing for its mother. His eyelids flickered; what dream was the poor boy having? I didn't know whether to wake him or let him be. The crying and twitching continued, and I also felt tears in my eyes. I gently called his name. Slowly, the cries died, and the twitches stopped. He lifted his head as he opened his eyes. He blinked, then sat bolt upright, looking around—a look of fear from waking from a deep sleep that he didn't know where he was. I gently called his name again but still allowed him space to settle before coming to him and gathering him up for a cuddle.

. . .

To read what happened next with Joey go to Amazon https://mybook.to/FBjApgU

Expectations when adopting a rescue

Whether you like to follow a specific breed or adopt a rescue dog, settling them and you into a life together is never straightforward. As humans, we have our expectations of what a puppy or an older dog will bring to our lives.

When I adopted Joey, I thought no more than a dog would be a good companion, that I would be giving him a good home and that I was responsible for his needs. In those days, there wasn't the 3 x 3 x 3 rule, which would have benefited us both.

What is the 3 x 3 x 3 rule?

Three days to decompress.

- They'll be feeling overwhelmed and confused.
- They may feel scared of what is going on.
- They may be withdrawn as they don't understand what is happening.
- They may hide and ignore you.
- They may test the boundaries in their new home.

Three weeks to learn a new routine.

- They will start to settle into their new home.
- Feel more comfortable.
- Start to feel more settled and believe this is their forever home.
- Settle into a new routine.
- Start to relax and show their personality.

Three months to feel at home.

- Finally, they feel they belong and are part of the family.
- Begin to trust and build a bond.
- Feel secure.
- Settles into their new life.

Joey, however cute and sweet he was, was a nightmare! I could understand that he was pining for his previous life. All I knew was that his owner had died, but at ten years old, he was totally confused, sad, and withdrawn. I think I made every mistake in the book in trying to encourage him to enjoy his new life. His barking in the car drove me bonkers. His escape attempts stressed me to the limits, but we persevered.

I don't think Joey felt comfortable for at least twelve months, even then, he still tried to escape!

Smudge, who we had from Immingham Dogs Home, was a different kettle of fish. We knew more about his past, which helped immensely, and, as David had been a dog foster parent in his previous life, we understood much more about adopting a rescue.

Smudge was and is a lot more confident. He had been well trained at some point, except on a lead! That is still a work in progress. Kelly told us that his crate was his safe place. Never having utilised a crate before other than for safety in the car for

Joey, this was alien to me. We duly got him his own crate, which he headed straight for when we brought him home.

If he goes into his crate, we know to leave him be. It's just like a teenager going to their room, I suppose. Smudge also enjoys going into my office [the dining room], usually in the evenings when we are both watching TV. More 'crate space' but on a larger scale!

It was important that Kelly and Smudge's foster mum were available to provide any advice we needed. They were both brilliant and helped immensely. Like Joey, I don't think Smudge truly settled until we had had him for about twelve months.

Eighteen months after his joining us, I like to think we are still learning about each other and enriching each other's lives.

Adoption Questions

When we see the dog we think we would like to adopt, our hearts leap. Rationality goes out the window, our brains turn to mush, and our hearts take the lead.

It's worth bearing in mind that some rescue centres may not know much about a dog's past, but they can give you helpful information to make you and your dog have a smoother transition into one happy family. After all, they have been around the dogs in the kennels, walking, cuddling, and feeding them, so they will have gained a lot of knowledge about their personalities and foibles.

Family members, from the children to visiting relatives, need to understand that a rescue dog coming into the family needs peace and quiet to start with. Not all dogs come with the confidence of our Smudge. Even he needed time to get used to new surroundings. Everyone needs to learn how to approach a new pet as they decompress.

Here are some helpful questions you could ask when the brain mush takes over.

All about dog

I am friendly with: -

People/Ladies/ Men/Young Children/Older Children

Dogs/ Cats/ Other

I am reactive to

I will react by

When I am at home

I am toilet-trained/I need some extra training/I am crate-trained

Once settled, I can be left alone for

I like to sleep

On the couch/On your bed/Crate, door closed/Crate, door open

My favourite toys are

Tennis balls/Squeakies/Soft toys/Footballs/Other.

Travelling

I travel well in a car/i am not good in a car

In a harness and safety lead on the rear seat

Secure in the tailgate/or a crate

When travelling,

I settle quickly/whine a little/bark/I'm sick/I get nervous.

Going to the vets and groomers

I enjoy the experience/I can be snappy

Food

I eat the following

My meal times are currently

I gobble my food/I graze.

I like a regular bowl/Deep bowl/Slow feeder bowl/Plate.

I will beg/I will steal from other dogs/I will steal from humans

I am protective of my food

My favourite treats are

Walkies

I prefer. Lead and collar/harness/halti

I am good on a lead/pull/need work.

I ignore other dogs/nervous of them/like to say hello/bark/growl.

My favourite place to go walkies is

Commands I am good at

Sit/stay/down/wait/heel/leave/come/no/I need work

Add any other questions here that come into your mind.

How did the book get its title?

It's been great collating rescue stories from the Immingham Dogs Home adopters, and I didn't feel it was for me to bring them all together by creating the title. The only option was to get book title suggestions from the rescuers themselves, and they didn't let me down.

We had a great inpouring of loving titles from people, and I had to think long and hard to choose the one that seemed a good fit. I whittled it down to three and then the final one, '**Hold my lead, I've got a tail to tell**'. Having the advantage of reading all the stories, I felt this encompassed every single one.

Thank you to everyone who got their creative juices flowing.

Shakira We Adopted, not Shopped
The stories of our Immingham Dogs Home Rescues
How we met our Pawfect Match

Michelle There's no place like home [we found ours thanks to IDH]

You can't find love, but you can adopt

Jessica Happily Ever After

Rags to Riches

Jenny Happy Tails [stories of adopted dogs from IDH]

Furever Homes [adopted dog stories from IDH]

Helen I Now have a Life

Sally Paws for a Second; our new Furever Home Awaits

Furever Grateful, Rescued Dogs' Tails

Home at last

Hold my lead, I've got a tail to tell

Shelly A Reason to Rescue

A New Leash of Life

Home at Last

Love Unleashed

Trish A Furry Tail Ending

Bex Looking for a Pawfect Friend, Think Rescue

Steve Pawfect Endings

Eleanor Tails of Immingham Dogs Home happy endings

Charlotte Paws for Thought

Yappy Endings

A Dogs Home is where the Heart is

I Chews you

Lead me home

A Doggos Tail

Sit, Stay, Forevermore

[Tales of love and trust between rescued and rescuer]

Diane, I'm Home [Tails of the sad to the sweet life of an Immingham Dog]

Rosemary Happiness a Rescue can bring

Nick Forever Homed, a Dogs Story

Alison J Moore

Alison has travelled extensively in the UK all her life, originally with her parents in their caravan and later with her husband in a tent. Motorhoming called when age dictated it, and she enjoys travelling with her partner in comfort these days.

When the single life beckoned in her early forties, Alison bought her small village house in Lanjaron, Spain, with the idea of travelling between the two before moving there permanently after she had sold her design and print business in the UK. The split life suited her and gave her a quality of life she had never envisaged: peace, quiet, and relaxation. It was what she needed, and she cherished the rural community and her friends there.

Alison's books are all based on personal experiences and the memories evoked by them. Her book, 'Just Joey', who was her companion during most of her single life, is a tribute to her much-loved dog at the time.

Alison currently lives in the Lincolnshire Wolds, which differs greatly from her childhood in the Birmingham suburbs. In addition to writing, Alison is a keen crafter and artist. In between writing books, she loses herself in drawing pet portraits in coloured pencil.

For more information, please visit her website www.alisonjmoore.com

Printed in Great Britain
by Amazon

48994475R00099